PROBLEMS AND PERSPECTIVES IN HISTORY

EDITOR: H. F. KEARNEY MA PHD

From Bismarck to Hitler

PROBLEMS AND PERSPECTIVES IN HISTORY

EDITOR: H. F. KEARNEY MA PHD

A full list of titles in this series
will be found on the back cover of this book

Ich
führe Euch herrlichen Pleiten entgegen!

Adolf Hitler as Kaiser Wilhelm II; a photomontage by John Heartfield, August 1932

From Bismarck to Hitler

The Problem of Continuity
in German History

J. C. G. Röhl, M.A., Ph.D.

LECTURER IN HISTORY
UNIVERSITY OF SUSSEX

BARNES & NOBLE, Inc.
NEW YORK
PUBLISHERS & BOOKSELLERS SINCE 1873

95466

Published in the United States in 1970
by Barnes & Noble, Inc.
105 Fifth Avenue, New York

SBN 389 01359 5

FOR
FRANK MAKIN

Printed in Great Britain by Richard Clay (The Chaucer Press) Ltd.
Bungay, Suffolk

Editor's Foreword

'Study problems in preference to periods' was the excellent advice given by Lord Acton in his inaugural lecture at Cambridge. To accept it is one thing, to put it into practice is another. In fact, in both schools and universities the teaching of history, in depth, is often hindered by certain difficulties of a technical nature, chiefly to do with the availability of sources. In this respect, history tends to be badly off in comparison with literature or the sciences. The historical equivalents of set texts, readings or experiments, in which the student is encouraged to use his own mind, are the so-called 'special periods'. If these are to be fruitful, the student must be encouraged to deal in his own way with the problems raised by historical documents and the historiography of the issues in question and he must be made aware of the wider perspectives of history. Thus, if the enclosure movement of the sixteenth century is studied, the student might examine the historiographical explanations stretching from More's *Utopia* and Cobbett to Beresford's *Lost Villages of England*. At the same time he might also be dealing with selected documents raising important problems. Finally he might be encouraged to realize the problems of peasantries at other periods of time, including Russia and China in the nineteenth and twentieth centuries. In this particular instance, thanks to Tawney and Power, *Tudor Economic Documents*, the history teacher is comparatively well off. For other special periods the situation is much more difficult. If, however, the study of history is to encourage the development of the critical faculties as well as the memory, this approach offers the best hope. The object of this series is to go some way towards meeting these difficulties.

The general plan of each volume in the series will be similar, with a threefold approach from aspects of historiography, documents and editorial consideration of wider issues, though the structure and balance between the three aspects may vary.

A broad view is being taken of the limits of history. Political history will not be excluded, but a good deal of emphasis will be placed on economic, intellectual and social history. The idea has in fact grown out of the experience of a group of historians at the University of Sussex, where the student is encouraged to investigate the frontier areas between his own and related disciplines.

H. F. KEARNEY

*The appeal to national character is generally
a mere confession of ignorance.*
MAX WEBER

*Überall im Studium mag man mit den Anfängen
beginnen, nur bei der Geschichte nicht.*
JACOB BURCKHARDT

Contents

Acknowledgements

We are grateful to the following for permission to reproduce copyright material:

Author's agents for extracts from *An Ambassador of Peace* by Viscount D'Abernon; Edward Arnold (Publishers) Ltd. for extracts from *A Record of British Diplomacy* by Lord Newton and for extracts from *Germany and the Next War* by F. von Bernhardi; Atlantis Verlag for extracts from *The von Hassell Diaries 1938–1944*; F. Bruckmann Verlag for extracts from *Briefe, Volume II* by H. S. Chamberlain; Bundeszentrale für politische Bildung and Berto Verlag for extracts from *Germans Against Hitler* by Zimmerman and Jacobson; Cambridge University Press for an extract from an article by J. C. G. Rohl in *The Historical Journal*, Volume 12, Number 3; Chatto & Windus Ltd. and W. W. Norton & Co. Inc. for extracts from *Germany's Aims in the First World War* by Fritz Fischer, copyright 1961 by Droste Verlag und Druckerei GmbH and translation copyright 1967 by W. W. Norton & Co. Inc. and Chatto and Windus Ltd.; The Clarendon Press for extracts from *The Reichswehr and Politics 1918 to 1933* by F. L. Carsten; William Collins Sons & Co. Ltd. and Walter Verlag for extracts from *Die Anatomie des SS – Staates Vol. I* by Buchheim et al; Curtis Brown Ltd. for extracts from *Gustav Stresemann: His Diaries, Letters and Papers*, edited and translated by Eric Sutton; Joan Daves for an extract from *Der Nationalsozialismus Dokumente 1933–1945* by Walter Hofer, copyright 1957 by Fischer Bucherei KG and for an extract from *Dokumente zur Deutschen Politik* by Harry Pross, copyright 1963 by Fischer Bucherei KG; Andre Deutsch Ltd. for extracts from *Memoirs* by Franz von Papen; Deutsche Verlags-Anstalt GmbH for an extract from *Vierteljahreshefte Für Zeitgeschichte*, Volume 13, 1965; Droste Verlag and Druckerei GmbH for an extract from *Der Kapp-Luttwitz-Putsch* by J. Erger; the Proprietors of *Encounter* and the author for an extract from 'Stauffenberg's Bomb' by F. L. Carsten from *Encounter*, September 1964; Faber and Faber Ltd. and E. P. Dutton & Co. Inc. for an extract from *The Roots of National Socialism* by R. D. O. Butler; Fischer Bucherei GmbH for extracts from *Die Deutsche Revolution 1918–1919*, edited by G. A. Ritter and S. Miller; Foreign office for an extract from the Streseman

ACKNOWLEDGEMENTS

Papers; Guardian Newspapers Ltd. for extracts from the *Manchester Guardian*, December 12th 1917; Harvard University Press for extracts from *The German Catastrophe: Reflections and Recollections* by F. Meinecke, translated by S. B. Fay, copyright 1950 by the President and Fellows of Harvard College; William Heinemann Ltd. and G. P. Putnam's Sons for an extract from Heinrich Himmler by R. Manvell and H. Fraenkel, copyright 1965 by Roger Manvell and Heinrich Fraenkel; The Controller of Her Majesty's Stationery Office for extracts from *Documents on British Foreign Policy 1919–1939*, Third Series, Volume 7, *Documents on German Foreign Policy 1918–1945*, Series D, Volume I and *British Documents on the Origins of the War*, Appendix A; Macmillan & Co. Ltd., St. Martins Press Inc. and The Macmillan Co. of Canada Ltd. for an extract from *Hindenburg: The Wooden Titan* by H. W. Wheeler-Bennett; Methuen & Co. Ltd. for an extract from *Assize of Arms* by J. H. Morgan; John Murray (Publishers) Ltd. and E. P. Dutton & Co. Inc. for an extract from *Germany and England* by J. A. Cramb and John Murray (Publishers) Ltd. and Harper and Row for an extract from *Bismarck: His Reflections and Reminiscences*; Musterschmidt Verlag for an extract from Der Kaiser, edited by W. Gorlitz; William Reeves Ltd. for extracts from *Richard Wagner – Judaism in Music* translated by Edwin Evans; the Proprietors of *The Review of Politics* for extracts from 'Shirer's History of Nazi Germany' by K. Epstein from *The Review of Politics*, Volume 23, No. 2. April 1961; Ring Verlag for an extract from *Die Auflosung der Weimarer Republik* by K. D. Bracher; Alfred Scherz Verlag for an extract from *Deutschland zwischen Demokratie und Diktatur* by K. D. Bracher; Martin Secker & Warburg Ltd. and Simon & Schuster Inc. for extracts from *The Rise and Fall of the Third Reich* by William Shirer, copyright 1959 and 1960 by William L. Shirer; Siegfried Toeche-Mittler for an extract from *Politische Schriften und Reden* by Meinecke; International Council for Philosophy and Humanistic Studies for extracts from *The Third Reich*; Vandenhoeck & Ruprecht for an extract from *Lebenserinnerungen* by W. Groener; Weidenfeld & Nicolson Ltd. and Farrar, Straus & Giroux Inc. for extracts from *Hitler's Table Talk*, edited by H. Trevor-Roper, copyright 1953 by Farrar, Straus & Young, Inc., Weidenfeld & Nicolson Ltd. and Holt, Rinehart & Winston Inc. for extracts from *Tagebucher 1918–1937* by H. G. Kessler, copyright 1970 by Holt, Rinehart & Winston Inc. and Weidenfeld & Nicolson Ltd. and Harcourt, Brace & World Inc. for Table Two from *The German Economy, 1870 to the Present* by Gustav Stoolper; Georg Westermann Verlag for extracts from *Unsterbliches Deutschland* by F. Von des Goltz and T. Stiefenhofer.

We have been unable to trace the copyright holders of the following and would be grateful for any information that would enable us to do so: Extract from 'Motive and Taktik der Reichsleitung 1914' by E. Zechlin from Der Monat, Volume 209, February 1966; extract from *The Blood and Iron Chancellor* by L. Snyder; extract from *Das Ende Der Monarchie am 9 November 1918* by Kuno Graf von Westarp and extracts *Deutschlands Republikanische Reichsverfassung* by Hugo Preuss.

We are grateful to the following for permission to reproduce illustrations: Gertrud Heartfield for the frontispiece by John Heartfield; the Estate of George Grosz, Princetown, New Jersey, for *The White General* on page 118; Chatto and Windus Ltd. for permission to base the maps on pages 75 and 77 on ones that first appeared in F. Fischer, *German Aims in the First World War*, 1967, and to Seewald Verlag, Stuttgart, for permission to base the graph on page 128 on one that first appeared in G. Binder, *Epoche Der Entescheidungen*, 1960.

We have been unable to trace the copyright owners of material on pages 38, 132 and 133, and would appreciate any information that would enable us to do so.

The map on pages 132 and 133, based on an idea by Dr. A. Muatz, first appeared in the book, *Das Ende der Parteien*.

Introduction

It would probably be true to say that more books have been written about recent German history than about the modern history of any other country. In an age in which violence has assumed previously unknown proportions, the twelve years of Nazi terror still stand out as the most evil in world history, surpassing even Stalin's Great Terror of the 1930s. How and why the land of Goethe and Beethoven, of Marx and Einstein, sank to such depths is a question of burning interest by no means only to the specialist historian. It is a question which, perhaps more than any other, challenges the belief in human progress and in the existence – or at any rate the omnipotence – of God.

Historical scholarship has now reached the stage where few questions of importance remain to be answered about the rise of the Nazis and the nature of their rule from 1933 to 1945, but the problem of seeing the Nazi era in the wider perspective of German history remains acute. However, as research interest is coming to be concentrated more upon the years before 1918, as more is being learned about the aims of German leaders before and during the First World War, the theory of continuity in German history is gaining more and more currency as an explanation of Hitler's appeal to the German people.

Ironically, it was the Nazis themselves who first propagated the idea of continuity. It was they who claimed to be the spiritual descendants of the ancient Teutonic tribes, of Luther, Frederick the Great, Bismarck, Hindenburg and Ludendorff; they who invoked the ideas of Fichte and Jahn, Lagarde and Wagner, to justify their rule. The motive of Hitler and Goebbels in appealing to this tradition is not difficult to guess: it was to legitimize their régime. All the more remarkable, therefore, is the ready acceptance of the Nazi view of German history by the West and – after the embarrassing and disastrous episode of the Nazi–Soviet Pact – by Communist Russia when the Second World War broke out. *Their* motive in so doing was, of course, the very reverse: if Hitler had sought to claim the glory of Prussia for his dictatorship, the anti-German historians were saying that the Prussian tradition had culminated in the barbarism of the Third Reich.

Because both interpretations were so obviously propagandist in intention, they had become almost wholly discredited in academic circles by the end of the 1950s, and when the American journalist

William Shirer repeated these theories in 1960, he was severely censured by most historians in the West, as well as in Germany itself.

It was the work of a German historian, Professor Fritz Fischer of Hamburg University, which reopened the debate. The publication of his monumental study of Germany's aims in the First World War in 1961 aroused the greatest storm the German historical world has ever seen. Despite the initial outcry, his basic conclusions have now been widely accepted and his influence is clearly discernible in most of the monographs now appearing in Germany. Something of a historiographical revolution has occurred.

Fischer's investigations revealed a striking similarity between the official German war aims of the First World War and those pursued by Adolf Hitler, at least as far as their territorial extent was concerned. This strongly suggested that the two world wars had German ambitions at their core, and so made it possible to see German history from unification in 1871 to catastrophe in 1945 as a unified whole. However, many questions remained – and still remain – to be answered before such a view could gain general support.

The documents in Part Two of this volume are intended to provide introductory material on a number of the issues raised by Fischer's discoveries: to what extent were the seeds of German expansionism implanted in the Germany created by Bismarck in the years 1862–71 (Chapter I)? When did German leaders first feel that they had a mission to achieve 'world power' for Germany? What was the nature of Germany's aims in the First World War, and how did these aims differ from those pursued by the other belligerent powers (Chapter III)? Several of the key figures in the Weimar Republic – notably Stresemann and Seeckt – were leading annexationists in the First World War: how far had their aims changed after the defeat of 1918? Were the Allies wrong in treating Germany so harshly at the Peace of Versailles and after? Were they not thereby merely weakening the democratic forces in Germany and playing into the hands of nationalist fanatics like Hitler (Chapter V)? What were Hitler's aims and how do they compare with those of the First World War in which he had been a lance-corporal (Chapter VII)? And what were the foreign aims of the 'German establishment' – the men who helped Hitler into power in 1933 and tried to assassinate him eleven years later, on 20 July 1944 (Chapter VIII)?

Clearly, even if we confine our attention to foreign policy, a very complex picture will emerge. Bismarck's foreign aims were very different from those of Wilhelm II; those of Bethmann Hollweg differed from those of Tirpitz, or those of the younger Moltke, or those of Ludendorff. Stresemann's aims differed from Seeckt's, and both were very different from Hitler's. To apply the concept of continuity to them all, it would be necessary either to discount these differences and stress the common denominator, or alternatively to employ a definition of continuity which is sufficiently subtle to take the many differences into account. Some suggestions as to how this might be done are made at the end of this book.

If precise comparisons are relatively easy to make when dealing with the foreign policy of German statesmen, they are virtually impossible in the field of ideas or social change. It is now generally agreed that the method used by some writers, of stringing together selected passages from a number of German political theorists to construct a link with Nazi ideology, is academically unsound. The approach used in Chapter II, which deals with anti-Semitism in the reign of Kaiser Wilhelm II, is to examine the attitude of some of the men then in power to anti-Jewish ideas, rather than to analyse those ideas themselves.

Politically, the period from Bismarck to Hitler must be divided into three parts – the Empire, 1871–1918; the Republic, 1918–1933; and the Nazi era, 1933–45. Chapters IV and VI deal with the question of what actually changed in 1918 and 1933. To what extent did the old Imperial forces survive the revolution of 1918? What rôle did those forces play in the Weimar Republic, and how did their domestic aims differ from those of the revolutionary nationalist forces which eventually rallied to Hitler's standard? The last chapter, on the German opposition to Hitler, examines the internal aims of the German resistance movement.

The intention here is not, and cannot be, to 'cover' the entire period from 1871 to 1945, nor even to deal comprehensively with the continuity theory. It would be fascinating, for example, to trace the continuity of democratic traditions in Germany through the 1848 revolutions, the Prussian constitutional conflict of the 1860s, the Weimar years, to the establishment of the Federal Republic in 1949. This black-red-gold tradition in German history has often been in sharp conflict with the black-white-red tradition examined in this volume, and it deserves equal treatment if a balanced view is to be reached. The date 1871 is also problematic, and the student might feel the need to delve much further into the past. The two main components of Bismarck's compromise solution to the unification problem – German nationalism and Prussian expansionism – both had long histories behind them. At the same time, the traditions of separatism and particularism survived to play an extremely important rôle in German politics up to 1918 and beyond. The year 1945, on the other hand, seems to be a much clearer *caesura* in German history. The total military collapse, the massive population movements, the formal abolition by the Allies of the Prussian State, the occupation and division of Germany and the loss of the eastern territories, the collapse of the old social order and the rise of the Soviet Union and the United States – all this fundamentally transformed Germany's position at home and abroad, in a way in which it was not transformed in 1918. One sign of this transformation is the forthright manner in which German historians have recently been dealing with the German past.

Part One

THE ROOTS OF NATIONAL SOCIALISM

---

1 The Nazi View of German History 1936

FRIEDRICH FREIHERR VON DER GOLTZ
and THEODOR STIEFENHOFER

One day, perhaps, historians will recognize that Adolf Hitler's greatest achievement was to lead the German people to ultimate victory over the alien forces imposed upon them from outside, so forging us into a genuine nation at last.

Various starts in this direction had been made earlier – whenever, in fact, Providence gave the Germans a strong leader conscious of the peculiar German temper. In the First Reich, however, there were all too often long periods of weakness and misguided leadership. The forces working against the collection and invigoration of Germandom were too strong to permit these small beginnings to grow into something stronger, to enable the evolution towards nationhood to bear fruit. The triumph of the enemies of the German people seemed complete when the Congress of Vienna pushed a huge rock in front of the gate through which the Germans hoped to pass to national self-determination, freedom and unity. But Bismarck pushed this rock aside with titanic strength after the citizens' revolt of 1848, the 'revolution in dressing-gown and slippers', had failed to achieve the same aim because of its disunity and lack of realism.

Bismarck gave us the Second Reich whose shining outline had already become visible against the dark backcloth of Germany's miserable and impotent petty States in the rise of Prussia from Frederick the Great onwards. The Hohenzollern State was strengthened in its historical mission by the revival of a German national consciousness directed against the alien elements which had entered all aspects of German life after the Peace of Westphalia. At first this was admittedly

I

only a movement to halt the deterioration of Germany's cultural heritage and to free the national spirit and national culture from all un-German elements. But in time very definite political aims did evolve from this cultural movement. National unity and a unified state became the aim of the best Germans. It was of course no accident that as Prussia heroically rose to become one of Europe's great powers there occurred an upsurge of the German spirit in art and science, with German poetry in particular gaining world-wide recognition. The State-building Prussians derived valuable spiritual and moral support from these sources, too.

The Second Reich had a brief but brilliant history in the course of which it transformed itself from a continental military State into a State with world-wide commercial interests. It finally collapsed under the overwhelming attack of a hostile world, after achievements on the battlefield and at home that surpassed anything ever realized by any other nation since time began. It is instructive for all future generations to note, however, that this tragic end was brought on not by the overpowering might of our enemies, nor by the blockade which cut off our food supply, but solely by our internal collapse. To be sure – the German people could have been defeated by the 29 States (including Poland and Czechoslovakia) with a total population of 1,391,600,000 and about 44 million soldiers ranged against them. Perhaps it really was beyond their power to bring home the banner of victory from a fight to the death against such overwhelming odds, though the incomparable German soldier very nearly brought off even this miracle. But that our failure to achieve ultimate military victory turned into a catastrophe which destroyed the power and the glory of the Kaiser's Reich as well as our honour and well-being can surely only be explained by the fact that in November 1918 we were not a real 'nation', that is, a politically united people. Such a people would have gathered around its leaders and risen for the last desperate effort as soon as the vindictive terms of the armistice became known. A united nation would have forced the hate-filled enemy to concede better peace terms than a people torn by party strife and ready to stab the still unbeaten army in the back was capable of doing.

The Second Reich collapsed primarily because it was a State without full national support (*ein Staat ohne Staatsvolk*).

To have brought this state of affairs to an end, to have shown the Germans how they can give full support to the State and so become a nation – that is the true meaning of Adolf Hitler's leadership.

In the new Germany the people shall penetrate the State and the State the people, down to the smallest detail of their lives. The State shall take responsibility for the people and the people for the State. And together they shall carry on their strong shoulders -- our Immortal Germany . . .

In this task we constantly derive new encouragement and new inspiration from Germany's history. We see the *völkisch* line which stretches from Arminius through Henry I, Luther, the great Prussian kings, Stein and Bismarck to Adolf Hitler, and we nurse the steadfast belief that it will continue to stretch into a brilliant future so long as the German people remain at all times, in fortune and misfortune, in good days and bad -- for these will not be lacking -- a nation pledged to pull together, whatever fate has in store for it.

And of one thing we are certain: the turning-point in German history will become a turning-point for the whole world!

Unsterbliches Deutschland. G. Westermann, 1936, pp. 45–59.

2 The War-time Western View, 1941

ROHAN D'O. BUTLER

When the theory of National Socialism is viewed in relation to German political thought of the last century and a half it is seen to be stale stuff, stale and adulterated. It would be penance without profit to dissect the turgid unoriginality of Adolf Hitler and Alfred Rosenberg, and of their lesser company, Günther in racial theory, Darré in agriculture, and Feder in economics. The stress and presentation are novel perhaps, but the matter is hardly more than repetition. The exaltation of the heroic leader goes back through Moeller van den Bruck, Spengler, Lamprecht, Chamberlain, Nietzsche, Lassalle, Rodbertus and Hegel, back to Fichte's *Zwingherr zur Deutschheit*. The racial myth is only the latest edition of Spengler, Chamberlain, Lagarde, Dühring, Schemann, Wagner, Gobineau, and the adumbrations of Görres, Arndt and Jahn. In their anti-Semitism the Nazis have merely followed Dühring in theorizing a very widespread German prejudice which goes back to the Junker following of Marwitz and beyond. The concept of the all-significant totalitarian State was cherished in one form or another as early as Schelling and Adam Müller. The idea of the ruling élite occurs again and again in German thought from the time when the romantics proclaimed their faith in aristocracy. The community of the folk runs from Hitler right back to Herder. The full programme of economic autarky was outlined by Fichte in 1800. National Socialism itself derives in theory from Moeller van den Bruck, Spengler, Rathenau, Naumann, Dühring, Lassalle, Rodbertus, Fichte. There is hardly a thinker in the line who was not more or less a nationalist. Spengler foretold intensive nationalist propaganda; more than a century before, Herder and Novalis were urging it. The tradition of militarism – Banse, Bernhardi, Treitschke, Moltke, Ranke, Clausewitz – is only the reflection of Prusso-German history since Frederick II and before. The dynamic originality of German culture in contrast to the artificial civilization of the west was a theme dear to Moeller van den Bruck, Spengler, Mann, Chamberlain, Lagarde, Ranke, Fichte and the romantic school at large. The polemic against reason and the intellect is Nazi, neo-romantic, romantic. The supernational mission of German culture was evident to Novalis and Fichte as it is to Hitler and his followers. Living-space for Germans was the demand of Moeller van den Bruck, Bernhardi, Naumann, Ratzel and List. Pan-Germanism was already a cult with Arndt and Görres and Grimm. Law that is folk-law was a concept familiar to Savigny. The abasement of the individual before the State finds precedent with Hegel. The Nazis say that might is right; Spengler said it; Bernhardi said it; Nietzsche said it; Treitschke had said as much; so had Haller before him; so had Novalis.

It is a long line, long yet compact. And in it only the major figures have been noticed; and hardly all of them. For it is better to dwell a little upon the more important figures rather than to give a breathless and insipid record of the very many second-raters and disciples: especially so in German thought, the home of dreary scholiasts and intellectual hangers-on. There is scarcely one of the thinkers previously mentioned who was not famous in his own time or after it, often both; who was not eagerly studied by thousands and taken for granted by more.

It would, however, be patently inaccurate to regard this line of German thought as an entirely compact and original national whole, sufficient to and in itself – quite apart from the obvious fact that many of the theorists differed considerably among themselves, and that in any case the Nazi leaders can hardly be said to owe their power primarily to especial capacity and research in the field of intellectual theory. The rise and triumph of national socialism is certainly not fully explicable unless it is realized how very much its outlook was an extension of the traditional outlook of Germany; but at the same time appreciation of this factor should not prevent recognition of the cardinal importance of other more immediate factors in that ascendancy, of the personalities of Adolf Hitler, his followers and opponents, of prevailing economic conditions, of the politico-social complex of events which afforded the Nazis such scope.

The Roots of National Socialism. Faber and Faber, 1941, pp. 276 ff.

3 The German Catastrophe, 1946

FRIEDRICH MEINECKE

This, the first post-war German attempt to explain Nazism, is marked by bewilderment and despair, but also by a willingness to move far into the German past to look for the wrong turning.

In the Prussian state of Frederick William I and Frederick the Great there lived two souls, one capable of culture and the other hostile to culture. The Prussian army as created by Frederick William I brought forth a remarkably penetrating militarism that influenced all civil life and found its like in no neighbouring State. However, as early as the travel sketches of Montesquieu, who lived in Hanoverian territory near the Prussian frontier, we find some unpleasant things about it. . . .

As long as the synthesis of intellect and power seemed to look hopeful in the nineteenth century, we regarded even militarism with a more benevolent eye; we emphasized the undoubtedly high moral qualities which were evident in it; the iron sense of duty, the ascetic strictness in service, the disciplining of the character in general. Easily overlooked, however, was the fact that this disciplining developed a levelling habit of conformity of mind which narrowed the vision and also often led to a thoughtless subserviency towards all higher authorities. This habit of conformity caused many of the richer springs of life to dry up. Furthermore, the advocates of Prussian militarism overlooked at first the fact that all sorts of unlovely practices and passions could rage under cover of exterior discipline. Public life also might suffer from these effects of militarism if the statesmen and generals, who had grown comfortably important in the militarist atmosphere, had an influence on the life of the nation. This evil seemed apparent even at the time of the War of Liberation, when the synthesis of intellect and State was for the first time boldly attempted. The synthesis was in many ways brilliantly attested, but ultimately was fatally crippled by a militarily narrow-minded monarch and by an equally narrow-minded and at the same time egotistical caste of nobles and officers. The crippling of the reform movement, symbolized in 1819 by the dismissal of Wilhelm von Humboldt and Boyen, may be regarded as a victory in the Prussian State of the soul that was hostile to culture over the soul that was capable of culture. The rift ran straight through the whole nineteenth century and was inherited by the twentieth century. Finally, Prussian militarism also secured a large place for itself in the mixing pot into which Adolf Hitler threw together all substances and essences of German development which he found usable.

However, in the era when the Empire was founded, the aspects of Prussian militarism which were bad and dangerous for the general well-being were obscured by the imposing proof of its power and discipline in its service for national unity and in the construction of Bismarck's Empire. The military man now seemed to be a consecrated spirit – the lieutenant moved through the world as a young god and the civilian reserve lieutenant at least as a demigod. He had to rise to be reserve officer in order to exert his full influence in the upper-middle class world and above all in the State administration. Thus militarism penetrated civilian life. Thus there developed a conventional Prussianism (*Borussismus*), a naïve self-admiration in the Prussian character, and together with it a serious narrowing of intellectual and political outlook. Everything was dissolved into a rigid conventionalism. One must have observed this type in countless examples with one's own eyes in the course of a long life, one must have felt it in one's own self, struggled with it, and gradually liberated one's self from it, in order to understand its power over men's minds – in order to understand finally the effect of the touching comedy in the Potsdam church on 21 March 1933, which Hitler prayed with Hindenburg beside the tomb of Frederick the Great. For here National Socialism was expected to appear as the heir and propagator of all the great and beautiful Prussian traditions. . . .

This evil Borussism and militarism was like a heavy mortgage imposed on Bismarck's work and inherited from him by his hybrid successor, Hitler. There was, however, also something in the immediate contribution of Bismarck himself which lay on the border between good and evil and which in its further development was to expand more on the side of evil. The truth of this criticism would never be readily conceded by those who grew great under Bismarck's work and richly enjoyed its blessings. We Germans often felt so free and proud, in contrast with the whole previous German past, in this mightily flourishing Empire of 1871 which gave living space to every one of us! But the staggering course of the First World War and still more of the Second World War makes it impossible to pass over in silence the query whether the germs of the later evil were not really implanted in Bismarck's work from the outset. It is a query which courageous and unfettered historical thinking must pose in regard to every great and apparently beneficent historical phenomenon in which a degeneration takes place. One then breathes the atmosphere of the tragedy of history, of human and historical greatness, and also the problematical uncertainty which will ever hover around a Bismarck and his work – while Hitler's work must be reckoned as the eruption of the Satanic principle in world history.

The German Catastrophe: reflections and recollections. Translated by Sidney B. Fay. Boston, Beacon Press, 1963, pp. 9 ff.

4 National Socialism and the German Past, 1955

GERHARD RITTER

The most outspoken attack on the various attempts to link Hitler with the Prussian past was made by the 'grand master' of German historians, the late Professor Ritter (1888–1967), who was a member of the German resistance movement against Hitler.

The Germans themselves were more surprised than anyone else by the rapid rise of the National Socialist Party to a position in which overall power in the State was at its disposal. Up to 1930 the vast majority of educated Germans thought Hitler's disciples to be a group of loud-mouthed extremists and super-patriots without any practical importance. The theatricality of their processions and meetings, the strangeness of their uniforms and of their bright red banners might awaken the curiosity of a tasteless crowd or seduce the more vulgar lower-middle class members of the large towns; but it all seemed absurd to educated people, who were horrified by the brutality of the Brown Shirts, by the disturbances which they made at meetings, and by their nocturnal thuggery in the streets. . . .

After 1923 the Hitlerian movement, too, seemed to have had its day. At the elections to the fourth Reichstag of the Republic in 1928 it gained only 2·6 per cent of the total votes; there were only twelve National Socialist deputies out of a total of 491. No one would have thought the sudden increase to 18·3 per cent in the September 1930 elections possible – and no one thought so less than the Brüning Government when it pronounced the dissolution of the fourth Reichstag a short time earlier.

It was only from this time on that Hitler's movement was taken seriously. . . .

All agreed, however, that the actual Hitlerian movement was not yet ripe, and that it must be regarded as the result of the effervescence of troubled times – all agreed not to take its leaders and its programme quite seriously. Even after the seizure of power on 30 January 1933 it was thought that the new régime could not last long. Many Germans were unwilling to believe that so civilized a people would let themselves be governed for long by such 'barbarian', and eccentric men, or that they would bear with Adolf Hitler's dictatorship for more than a short time. . . .

Hitler himself never sought a restoration; he sought its opposite. He thought that the patriotism of conservative *milieux* looked towards the past, was out of date, and absurdly inefficient as regards mass propaganda. . . . Hitler's propaganda was based not on the memory of 'our forefathers' deeds', but on an indomitable will for the future. His State was to be completely new, something that had never before been seen, contemporary and modern, a State that could be created only once. He poured criticism and scorn on the institutions which existed under a hereditary monarchy under which the ultimate orders were made not by the most able, but by those in power on account of an accident of birth and of heredity, as he said in private. But in public, in his propaganda, for as long as he needed the support of conservative groups (national Germans), he expressed no such views. In fact, the only thing which he had in common with the monarchists was his opposition to the Weimar system, and only such fanatical, blind, and single-minded people as the German conservatives (Hugenberg's followers) could be unaware of, or ignore, how far his attitude was revolutionary and anti-monarchist. The fact that a few German princes wished to support him is explicable only because Court circles, in which the opinions of the people were unknown, left them completely devoid of instinct. Hitler did not regard himself as a member of the upper classes, but as a common man, a people's leader (*Volksführer*) in the most radical demo-cratic manner – the direct representative of democratic principles, the representative of the will of the people, the 'only delegate of the nation' as he often described himself in his 'leader's speeches' (*Führerreden*).

It is a very great mistake to believe that the modern function of leader of the people is in any way the heritage and continuation of the old, monarchic power of the princes. Neither Frederick the Great, Bismarck, nor Wilhelm II were the historical precursors of Adolf Hitler. His precursors were the demagogues and Caesars of modern history, from Danton to Lenin and Mussolini.

The Third Reich: Essays published under the auspices of the Inter-national Council for Philosophy and Humanistic Studies and with the assistance of UNESCO. Weidenfeld and Nicolson, 1955, pp. 381 ff.

5 The Historical Roots of the Third Reich, 1960

WILLIAM L. SHIRER

Shirer's account of the historical origins of Nazism revived wartime notions on the course of German history. Not a professional historian but a journalist, Shirer worked as a correspondent in Germany between 1926–41.

In the delirious days of the annual rallies of the Nazi Party at Nuremberg at the beginning of September, I used to be accosted by a swarm of hawkers selling a picture postcard on which were shown the portraits of Frederick the Great, Bismarck, Hindenburg and Hitler. The inscription read: 'What the King conquered, the Prince formed, the Field-Marshal defended, the Soldier saved and unified'. Thus Hitler, the soldier, was portrayed not only as the saviour and unifier of Germany but as the successor of these celebrated figures who had made the country great. The implication of the continuity of German history, culminating in Hitler's rule, was not lost on the multitude. The very expression 'the Third Reich' also served to strengthen this concept. The First Reich had been the medieval Holy Roman Empire; the second had been that which was formed by Bismarck in 1871 after Prussia's defeat of France. Both had added glory to the German name. The Weimar Republic, as Nazi propaganda had it, had dragged that fair name in the mud. The Third Reich restored it, just as Hitler had promised. Hitler's Germany, then, was depicted as a logical development from all that had gone before – or at least all that had been glorious. . . .

Acceptance of autocracy, of blind obedience to the petty tyrants who ruled as princes, became ingrained in the German mind. The idea of democracy, of rule by parliament, which made such rapid headway in England in the seventeenth and eighteenth centuries, and which exploded in France in 1789, did not sprout in Germany. This political backwardness of the Germans, divided as they were into so many petty States and isolated in them from the surging currents of European thought and development, set Germany apart from and behind the other countries of the West. There was no natural growth of a nation. This has to be borne in mind if one is to comprehend the disastrous road this people subsequently took and the warped state of mind which settled over it. In the end the German nation was forged by naked force and held together by naked aggression.

Beyond the Elbe to the east lay Prussia. As the nineteenth century waned, this century which had seen the sorry failure of the confused and timid liberals at Frankfurt in 1848–9 to create a somewhat demo-cratic, unified Germany, Prussia took over the German destiny. For centuries this Germanic State had lain outside the main stream of German historical development and culture. It seemed almost as if it were a freak of history. Prussia had begun as the remote frontier state of Brandenburg on the sandy wastes east of the Elbe which, beginning with the eleventh century, had been slowly conquered from the Slavs. Under Brandenburg's ruling princes, the Hohenzollerns, who were little more than military adventurers, the Slavs, mostly Poles, were gradually pushed back along the Baltic. Those who resisted were either exterminated or made landless serfs. . . .

By this time [1701] Prussia had pulled itself up by its own bootstraps to be one of the ranking military powers in Europe. It had none of the resources of the others. Its land was barren and bereft of minerals. The population was small. There were no large towns, no industry and little culture. Even the nobility was poor, and the landless peasants lived like cattle. Yet by a supreme act of will and a genius for organization the Hohenzollerns managed to create a Spartan military State whose well-drilled army won one victory after another and whose Machiavellian diplomacy of temporary alliances with whatever power seemed the strongest brought constant additions to its territory.

There thus arose quite artificially a State born of no popular force nor even of an idea except that of conquest, and held together by the absolute power of the ruler, by a narrow-minded bureaucracy which did his bidding and by a ruthlessly disciplined army. Two-thirds and sometimes as much as five-sixths of the annual State revenue was expended on the army, which became, under the King, the State itself. 'Prussia', remarked Mirabeau, 'is not a State with an army, but an army with a State.' And the State, which was run with the efficiency and soullessness of a factory, became all; the people were little more than cogs in the machinery. Individuals were taught not only by the kings and the drill sergeants but by the philosophers that their rôle in life was one of obedience, work, sacrifice and duty. Even Kant preached that duty demands the suppression of human feeling, and the Prussian poet Willibald Alexis glories in the enslavement of the people under the

Hohenzollerns. To Lessing, who did not like it, 'Prussia was the most slavish country in Europe.'

The Junkers, who were to play such a vital rôle in modern Germany, were also a unique product of Prussia. They were, as they said, a master race. It was they who occupied the land conquered from the Slavs and who farmed it on large estates worked by these Slavs, who became landless serfs quite different from those in the west. There was an essential difference between the agrarian system in Prussia and that of western Germany and western Europe. In the latter, the nobles, who owned most of the land, received rents or feudal dues from the peasants, who though often kept in a state of serfdom had certain rights and privileges and could, and did, gradually acquire their own land and civic freedom. In the west, the peasants formed a solid part of the community; the landlords, for all their drawbacks, developed in their leisure a cultivation which led to, among other things, a civilized quality of life that could be seen in the refinement of manners, of thought and of the arts.

The Prussian Junker was not a man of leisure. He worked hard at managing his large estate, much as a factory manager does today. His landless labourers were treated as virtual slaves. On his large estates he was the absolute lord. There were no large towns nor any substantial middle class, as there were in the west, whose civilizing influence might rub against him. In contrast to the cultivated *grand seigneur* in the west, the Junker developed into a rude, domineering, arrogant type of man, without cultivation or culture, aggressive, conceited, ruthless, narrow-minded and given to a petty profit-seeking that some German historians noted in the private life of Otto von Bismarck, the most successful of the Junkers.

It was this political genius, this apostle of 'blood and iron', who between 1866 and 1871 brought an end to a divided Germany which had existed for nearly a thousand years and, by force, replaced it with Greater Prussia, or what might be called Prussian Germany. Bismarck's unique creation is the Germany we have known in our time, a problem child of Europe and the world for nearly a century, a nation of gifted, vigorous people in which first this remarkable man and then Kaiser Wilhelm II and finally Hitler, aided by a military caste and by many a strange intellectual, succeeded in inculcating a lust for power and domination, a passion for unbridled militarism, a contempt for democracy and individual freedom and a longing for authority, for authoritarianism. Under such a spell, this nation rose to great heights, fell and rose again, until it was seemingly destroyed with the end of Hitler in the spring of 1945 – it is perhaps too early to speak of that with any certainty.

The Rise and Fall of the Third Reich: A History of Nazi Germany. Secker and Warburg, 1960, pp. 90 ff.

6 An Attack on Shirer, 1961

KLAUS EPSTEIN

Epstein had emigrated from Germany as a young boy, and had established himself as one of the leading American historians of Germany when he was tragically killed in a car accident in Bonn in 1967, leaving his massive work on German conservatism uncompleted. Noted above all for his brilliant reviews, Epstein had little difficulty in scoring heavily off Shirer.

William Shirer's *Rise and Fall of the Third Reich: A History of Nazi Germany* has been widely hailed as a great work of history. Harry Schermann, chairman of the board of directors of the Book of the Month Club, says that it 'will almost certainly come to be considered the definitive history of one of the most frightful chapters in the story of mankind.' The book has already sold more widely than any work on European history published in recent years. It is probable that tens of thousands of American readers will take their views on recent German affairs from Shirer's pages for years to come. For that reason, it is important to point out the serious shortcomings of this work. I believe it suffers from four major failings: (1) Its overall conception of German history is unbelievably crude, and precludes the author from asking many of the most important questions that need to be answered about the Nazi period. (2) The book is completely lacking in overall balance; it is marred by glaring gaps in precisely those areas of the Nazi record where new research is most urgently needed. (3) Many of Shirer's interpretations show a curious inability to understand the nature of a modern totalitarian régime. (4) The book is in no way abreast of current scholarship dealing with the Nazi period. It is the purpose of this review article to substantiate these severe charges. . . .

Shirer . . . is convinced that there is a specific logic which governs the course of German development and that he possesses the key to that logic. German history from 1871 to 1945 runs 'in a straight line and with utter logic'. Nazism is 'but a logical continuation of German history'. He frequently talks about the German national character, which he believes to have been shaped by such miscellaneous factors as the long experience of disunity, a penchant for sadism (and masochism), and Germany's general backwardness. Some of his judgements in connection with the latter point reveal much ignorance and prejudice. Shirer states, for example, that Germany was reduced, after the Peace of Westphalia in 1648, 'to the barbarism of Muscovy'. But where is the Russian Leibnitz of the next generation? Shirer's view of the Hohenzollerns is as follows: 'Under Brandenburg's ruling princes, the Hohenzollerns, who were little more than military adventurers, the Slavs, mostly Poles, were gradually pushed back along the Baltic'. This statement is mistaken on several grounds. Anybody possessing the slightest familiarity with German medieval history knows that the *Drang nach Osten*, which gradually pushed the Slavs back along the Baltic, was completed well before 1400, whereas the Hohenzollerns became margraves of Brandenburg only in 1417. To refer to the Hohenzollerns as 'little more than military adventurers' does little credit to Shirer's knowledge of Prussian history. Frederick I (1417–40) was one of the greatest German princes of the fifteenth century. Joachim I (1499–1535) founded the University of Frankfurt and was instrumental in the reception of Roman Law. Joachim II (1535–71) introduced the Reformation and reorganized the entire administrative structure of his State. The Great Elector (1640–88) was one of the most versatile rulers of his age, a vigorous mercantilist, a patron of culture, and a great administrator, in short the very antithesis of a military adventurer. I will charitably assume that Shirer's statement was intended to apply only to the early Hohenzollerns – it is even more patently absurd when applied to Frederick I, Frederick William I, Frederick the Great, etc. Shirer's ignorance about Prussia is complemented by strong prejudices on that subject – leading him to general accusations which include statements such as that 'even Kant preached that duty demands the suppression of human feeling . . .'. Did Socrates in fact teach anything else?

Shirer accuses not only the German middle class but also the working class of trading 'for material gain any aspirations for political freedom they may have had', with Bismarck's social legislation having 'a profound influence on the working class in that it gradually made them value security over political freedom and caused them to see in the State, however conservative, a benefactor and a protector'. Bismarck himself would have been most surprised by this indirect compliment to a policy which is generally held to have been a failure. Another sweeping thought-killing generalization is the following: 'They (the German middle class) accepted the Hohenzollern autocracy. They *gladly* knuckled under to the Junker bureaucracy and they *fervently* embraced Prussian militarism. Germany's star had risen and they – almost all the people – were *eager* to do what their masters asked to keep it high' (my italics). One can only ask: did the readers of the *Frankfurter Zeitung*, Germany's great liberal newspaper, belong to this kind of a homogeneous middle class? Shirer obviously does not have the slightest idea of the extent and vigour of the criticism which Left Liberals and Socialists continually delivered against the ruling group, military and civilian, of Wilhelmian Germany. He might profitably study the *Reichstag* debates in the *Daily Telegraph* (November 1908) or the Saverne Incidents (December 1913) – to mention only two examples – to correct his unbalanced view of German pre-war political life.

Shirer's one-sided misjudgements on Germany's political history appear relatively insignificant when compared with his systematic prejudice when dealing with Germany's cultural heritage. Hitler's *Weltanschauung* 'has its roots deep in German history and thought', more specifically in 'that odd assortment of erudite but unbalanced philosophers, historians and teachers who captured the German mind during the century before Hitler'. Shirer traces the pedigree of Nazism back to Fichte (described as delivering his nationalist Addresses 'from the podium of the University of Berlin' in 1807), Hegel (because he glorified the State and the hero), Treitschke (because he preached Prussianism and war), Nietzsche (because he gloried in elitism and expressed contempt for Christianity), and Wagner (whose world of 'the barbaric, pagan Nibelungs . . . has always fascinated the German mind and answered some terrible longing in the German soul'). Shirer adds Gobineau and Houston S. Chamberlain to this list of the precursors of Nazism while regretting that 'the limitations of space in a work of this kind prohibited discussion of the considerable influence on the Third Reich of a number of other German intellectuals whose writings were popular and significant in Germany: Schlegel, J. Goerres, Novalis,

Arndt, Jahn, Lagarde, List, Droysen, Ranke, Mommsen, Constantin Frantz, Stöcker, Bernhardi, Klaus Wagner, Langbehn, Lange, Spengler'. This grab-bag miscellany of names is unlikely to give the informed reader a favourable view of Shirer's mastery of German intellectual history. Shirer documents his one-sided theme by presenting parallel passages from Hitler, Hegel and Nietzsche. It is superfluous to comment on this crude throwback to wartime pamphleteering. Shirer falls into every one of the frequently exposed fallacies of his predecessors in the field of Nazi pedigree-hunting (McGovern, Viereck, Rohan O'Butler [sic], etc.): (1) exaggerating the specificity of the influence exercised by any so-called precursor; (2) extracting from the works of any so-called precursor those quotations which in some way anticipate Nazism, even though they may be a relatively unimportant element in the total corpus of an author's thought; (3) identifying Germany's intellectual heritage with a line of selected precursors, while ignoring those figures – however important in their own age (for example, Goethe) who do not fit into such a pedigree; (4) ignoring 'proto-Nazi thinkers' in non-German lands (for example, Carlyle or Danilevsky) whose existence throws considerable doubt upon a German uniqueness in this respect. The result of Shirer's kind of history is a garbled *ad hoc* presentation of the German heritage drawn up to prove what is clearly an *a priori* case. Shirer wants to prove that Hitler 'found in the German people, as a mysterious Providence and centuries of experience had moulded them up to that time (1933), a natural instrument which he was able to shape to his own sinister ends'.

The trouble with this kind of approach is not only that it distorts history, but it prevents a man who believes in it from asking many important questions about Nazism. Shirer never asks why there was so little popular resistance to the Nazi accession to power in 1933. He simply does not recognize this as a problem, for the entire German heritage made it inevitable – in his view – that Germans should greet Nazism enthusiastically. He does not ask: What went wrong with the German Socialists, once formidable and courageous champions of liberty? Or the Zentrum which had resisted Bismarck so heroically? Or the liberal section of the bourgeoisie, which had rallied to the Republic in 1918? The reader will vainly look in Shirer's book for answers to these problems.

'Shirer's History of Nazi Germany', *The Review of Politics*, **23**, No. 2, April 1961, pp. 230 ff.

Part Two

FROM BISMARCK TO HITLER

I

The Germany of Bismarck

Why begin with Bismarck? The limited nature of the three wars he fought to unify Germany in 1864, 1866 and 1870, the restraint he exercised in his treatment of Austria after the battle of Königgrätz, his refusal to establish a truly unified Reich, and his repeated assertion after 1871 that Germany was satiated – all this makes him appear more like a latter-day Metternich than a forerunner of Ludendorff and Hitler. It is not Bismarck's personality so much as his work that is at issue in the continuity debate. When the Democrat Max Weber made his famous statement in 1895, to the effect that Bismarck's unification would be judged as an irresponsible prank unless it provided the jumping-off point for further expansion, he was saying that the move from Bismarck's limited *Realpolitik* to Kaiser Wilhelm II's *Weltpolitik* lay in the logic of the Bismarckian Reich. By the war of 1870 against France, and the annexation of Alsace and Lorraine, the new Reich achieved a position of 'latent hegemony' in Europe. The danger that the defeated powers (Denmark, Austria-Hungary, France, the Vatican) and the powers who were disquieted by the new giant in the heart of Europe (Great Britain and Russia) would form a coalition to 'contain' Germany at the first sign of further expansionist tendencies, was therefore never far from the surface. In this position, German statesmen could pursue one of three courses: to refrain completely from further expansion while at the same time sowing discord among the other powers in order to persuade them to seek Germany's aid, which was the course pursued by Bismarck; to partition Austria-Hungary between Russia and Germany, which was advocated by a number of German leaders but did not become official policy before 1918; or to turn the 'latent hegemony' into full hegemony, so freeing Germany from restraint, which was the course favoured by extremists like Lagarde, and also at times by the Prussian army. As the German population and German industrial output outstripped that of her neighbours, and as a new generation, less aware of the dangers than Bismarck, rose to power, Bismarckian restraint became ever more unpopular.

1 Bismarck and the King at Nikolsburg in 1866

OTTO VON BISMARCK

After the victory of the Prussian troops over the Austrian army at Königgrätz, King Wilhelm I and the Prussian military leaders wanted to press on to impose a harsh peace with widespread territorial annexations on the enemy. Bismarck was alone in opposing the establishment of what he later, rather sarcastically, called 'an East Roman Empire' with its seat at Constantinople. He was already acutely aware of the danger of an anti-German coalition to 'contain' Germany. He did, however, consent to considerable annexations to Prussia in northern Germany. This is how he described his clash with the King in his memoirs, which were published on his death in 1898.

When it came to the point of dealing with Napoleon's telegram of 4 July [1866], the King had sketched out the conditions of peace as follows: a reform of the Federation under the headship of Prussia; the acquisition of Schleswig-Holstein, Austrian Silesia, a strip on the frontier of Bohemia, and East Friesland; the substitution of the respective heirs-apparent for the hostile sovereigns of Hanover, Electoral Hesse, Meiningen and Nassau. Subsequently other demands were advanced, which partly originated with the King himself, and were partly due to external influences. The King wished to annex parts of Saxony, Hanover, Hesse, and especially to bring Anspach and Baireuth again into the possession of his house. The reacquisition of the Franconian principalities touched his strong and justifiable family sentiment very nearly. . . .

On 23 July, under the presidency of the King, a council of war was held, in which the question to be decided was whether we should make peace under the conditions offered or continue the war. A painful illness from which I was suffering made it necessary that the council should be held in my room. On this occasion I was the only civilian in uniform. I declared it to be my conviction that peace must be concluded on the Austrian terms, but remained alone in my opinion; the King supported the military majority. My nerves could not stand the strain which had been put upon them day and night; I got up in silence,

walked into my adjoining bedchamber and was there overcome by a
violent paroxysm of tears. Meanwhile, I heard the council dispersing in
the next room. I thereupon set to work to commit to paper the reasons
which in my opinion spoke for the conclusion of peace; and begged the
King, in the event of his not accepting the advice for which I was
responsible, to relieve me of my functions as minister if the war were
continued. With this document I set out on the following day to explain
it by word of mouth. . . .

We had to avoid wounding Austria too severely; we had to avoid
leaving behind in her any unnecessary bitterness of feeling or desire for
revenge; we ought rather to reserve the possibility of becoming friends
again with our adversary of the moment, and in any case to regard the
Austrian State as a piece on the European chessboard and the renewal of
friendly relations with her as a move open to us. If Austria were
severely injured, she would become the ally of France and of every
other opponent of ours; she would even sacrifice her anti-Russian
interests for the sake of revenge on Prussia.

On the other hand, I could see no future acceptable to us for the
countries constituting the Austrian monarchy, in case the latter were
split up by risings of the Hungarians and Slavs or made permanently
dependent on those peoples. What would be put in that portion of
Europe which the Austrian state from Tyrol to the Bukowina had
hitherto occupied? Fresh formations on this surface could only be of a
permanently revolutionary nature. German Austria we could neither
wholly nor partly make use of. The acquisition of provinces like Austrian Silesia and portions of Bohemia could not strengthen the Prussian
State; it would not lead to an amalgamation of German Austria with
Prussia, and Vienna could not be governed from Berlin as a mere
dependency. . . . The resistance which I was obliged, in accordance with
my convictions, to offer to the King's views with regard to the following up of the military successes, and to his inclination to continue the
victorious advance, excited him to such a degree that a prolongation of
the discussion became impossible; and, under the impression that my
opinion was rejected, I left the room with the idea of begging the King
to allow me, in my capacity of officer, to rejoin my regiment. On
returning to my room I was in the mood that the thought occurred to
me whether it would not be better to fall out of the open window,
which was four storeys high; and I did not look round when I heard
the door open, although I suspected that the person entering was the
Crown Prince, whose room was in the same corridor I had just passed.

I felt his hand on my shoulder, while he said: 'You know that I was against this war. You considered it necessary, and the responsibility for it lies on you. If you are now persuaded that our end is attained, and peace must now be concluded, I am ready to support you and defend your opinion with my father.' He then repaired to the King, and came back after a short half-hour, in the same calm, friendly mood, but with the words: 'It has been a very difficult business, but my father has consented.' This consent found expression in a note written with lead pencil on the margin of one of my last memoranda, something to this effect: 'Inasmuch as my Minister-President has left me in the lurch in the face of the enemy, and here I am not in a position to supply his place, I have discussed the question with my son; and as he has associated himself with the Minister-President's opinion, I find myself reluctantly compelled, after such brilliant victories on the part of the army, to bite this sour apple and accept so disgraceful a peace.'

Bismarck, *His Reflections and Reminiscences*. London, Smith, Elder and Co., 1898, Vol. II, pp. 41 f., 47–52.

2 A New Element in Politics, 1870

JACOB BURCKHARDT

In a letter of 27 November 1870 the famous Swiss historian Jacob Burckhardt warned that, after the Franco-Prussian War, Europe would never again be at peace.

There is a new element in politics, a deepening, of which earlier victors knew nothing or at least made no conscious use. One is trying to humiliate the loser as much as possible, so that in future he will hardly dare to move. It is possible that this aim will be achieved; but whether one's own position will be the better and happier as a result is another question altogether.

O how the German nation errs if it thinks it will be able to put the rifle in one corner and turn to the arts and the happiness of peace! They will be told: above all you must continue your military training! And after a time no one will really be able to say what is the purpose of living. For soon the German–Russian war will loom on the horizon . . .

Briefe. Basel–Stuttgart, 1963, Vol. 5, pp. 111 f.

3 The German Revolution, 1871

BENJAMIN DISRAELI

Speech in the House of Commons, 9 February 1871.

. . . Now let me impress upon the attention of the House the character of this war. It is no common war, like the war between Prussia and Austria, or like the Italian war in which France was engaged some years ago; nor is it like the Crimean War. This war represents the German Revolution, a greater political event than the French Revolution of last century – I don't say a greater, or as great, a social event. What its social consequences may be are in the future. Not a single principle in the management of our foreign affairs, accepted by all statesmen for guidance up to six months ago, any longer exists. There is not a diplomatic tradition which has not been swept away. You have a new world, new influences at work, new and unknown objects and dangers with which to cope, at present involved in that obscurity incident to novelty in such affairs. We used to have discussions in this House about the balance of power . . . but what has really come to pass in Europe? The balance of power has been entirely destroyed, and the country which suffers most, and feels the effects of this great change most, is England.

Hansard's Parliamentary Debates, Third Series, Vol. CCIV, February–March 1871, pp. 81 f.

4 A New Iron Age, 1871

EDMUND JÖRG

Similar fears were expressed in Germany by the Catholic Democrat J. E. Jörg, writing on 1 January 1871.

The new German Kaiserdom has begun by adopting the Russian principle that all treaties are null and void as soon as they become uncomfortable to one of the parties, provided that it has the power to throw off the bothersome chains. . . .

One cannot assume from this that the near future will be peaceful; it would be more accurate to say: the more Kaiser we have the more war there will be. For our part, we have always kept in mind a simple test to distinguish the true from the untrue unification of Germany: the lowering or raising of the military burden. But who could possibly expect so much as the idea of disarmament to come from the new Reich?

The Kaiserdom of Bonaparte at least still contained dual elements; besides political nationalism there existed political tradition. The old order in Europe did not suit it, but it demanded a new order which was to be founded through European cooperation in a congress. Quite the opposite of the new German Kaiserdom. Born out of the terrible struggle with its western neighbour, it must from the start prohibit every sort of interference and mediation. As it claims to be a pure nation-State yet still incomplete nation-State, it cannot, by its very nature, accept that its boundaries be defined by binding treaties; it must rather reserve the right to pull into its framework at the next favourable opportunity those areas of German nationality which still stand outside it. Therefore it was no exaggeration but the truth when, months ago, it was proclaimed in Berlin that the new German Reich must be a *Weltreich*, strong enough to defeat, without alliances or treaties, not only any other power but a coalition of all foreign powers. . . .

How is one reasonably supposed to picture the future relationship of Germany and France, in view of the abyss of irreconcilable hatred which has opened up between them; how are the two nations to find their way back to each other while the whole French people passes on its grim thirst for revenge to its children and children's children?

From the military point of view the answer is simple, but unfortunately not very reassuring. From this point of view one can even arrive at the colossal idea that from now on France will have to be kept in check by the new German Reich as a vassal-State or fiefdom. About the other powers, whose initial sympathy has already turned into annoyance and distrust, one does not have to worry. If any of them raise objections they will be beaten down, in accordance with the new European order!

One thing, however, is certain: a political war between Prussia and France might have been concluded without essential changes in the general situation in Europe. But the national or racial war which has flared up between Germany and France changes everything, turns all relationships upside down and leads one to fear that the humanity and civilization of the nineteenth century will give way, in its final third, to a new Iron Age.

Die Reichsgründung, ed. Helmut Böhme, DTV, Munich, 1967, pp. 25 f.

5 The Objects of Bismarck's Policy, 1873–4

LORD ODO RUSSELL

The fears expressed in the foregoing passage, that Germany would again attack France and perhaps also Austria, to complete the work left undone in 1866 and 1871, were also shared by the British ambassador in Berlin, as these letters to the British ambassador in Paris show.

(*a*) Lord Odo Russell to Lord Lyons

British Embassy, Berlin,
14 March 1873

The two great objects of Bismarck's policy are:

1. The supremacy of Germany in Europe and of the German race in the world.

2. The neutralization of the influence and power of the Latin race in France and elsewhere.

To obtain these objects he will go any lengths while he lives, so that we must be prepared for surprises in the future. . . .

It appears to me that the re-establishment of the future balance of power in Europe on a general peace footing, is *the* thing Diplomacy should work for, and that nothing can be done so long as the Germans have not got their French gold, and the French got rid of their German soldiers.

The Germans, as you know, look upon the war of revenge as unavoidable and are making immense preparations for it.

Germany is in reality a great camp ready to break up for any war at a week's notice with a million of men. . . .

Thiers is again out of favour at Berlin, because the Russian Government has warned the German Government that Thiers is working to draw Russia into the Anglo-French Alliance contrary to their wishes. I believe myself that the alliance or understanding between Russia and Germany, Gortchakoff and Bismarck is real, intimate, and sincere; and that they have agreed to preserve Austria so long as she obeys and serves them, but woe to Austria if ever she attempts to be independent!

Then the German and Slav elements she is composed of, will be made to gravitate towards their natural centres, leaving Hungary and her dependencies as a semi-oriental vassal of Germany and Russia. However, those are things of the future.

Lord Newton, *Lord Lyons: A Record of British Diplomacy*. Edward Arnold, 1913, Vol. II, pp. 41 f.

(*b*) Lord Odo Russell to Lord Lyons

Berlin, 20 February 1874

I was glad after a long interval to see your handwriting again, and doubly glad to find you inclined to renew our correspondence. You ask: Firstly, What in my opinion should the French do to escape being attacked by Germany in their present defenceless state?

In my opinion nothing can save them *if* Bismarck is determined to fight them again; but then, is it France or is it Austria he is preparing to annihilate? In Bismarck's opinion, France, to avoid a conflict with him, should gag her press, imprison her bishops, quarrel with Rome, refrain from making an army or from seeking alliances with other powers all out of deference to Germany.

Secondly. What can other powers, and particularly England, do to help to preserve peace?

A coalition is impossible; advice or interference adds to Bismarck's excuses for going to war, so the only course Governments can follow is to let him do as he pleases and submit to the consequences, until he dies.

Thirdly. Do I attach any importance to the Emperor of Russia's pacific assurances?

None whatever, because Bismarck is prepared to buy his cooperation with anything he pleases in the East.

Bismarck is now master of the situation at home and abroad. The Emperor, the ministers, the army, the press, and the national majority in Parliament are instruments in his hands, while abroad he can so bribe the great powers as to prevent a coalition and make them subservient to his policy. Now, his policy, as you know, is to mediatize the minor States of Germany and to annex the German Provinces of Austria, so as to make one great centralized power of the German-speaking portions of Europe. To accomplish this he may require another war, but it may be with Austria and not with France, which he now puts forward to keep up the war spirit of the Germans and to remind Europe of his powers. Besides which he has to pass the unpopular Army Bill and War Budget which he failed in last summer.

Lord Newton, *Lord Lyons: A Record of British Diplomacy*, Vol. II, pp. 52 f.

6 The War-in-Sight Crisis of 1875

LORD ODO RUSSELL

In May 1875, the war between Germany and France which many had expected seemed about to break out. Though Bismarck represented France as the aggressor and urged the other powers to join Germany in preventing a French attack, he found to his dismay that a coalition arose to hold Germany in check.

(a) Lord Odo Russell to Lord Derby

Berlin, 1 May 1875

Since writing to you today, at this late hour my Belgian colleague Baron Nothomb has called to tell me that he had a long conversation with Moltke yesterday fully confirming what is said in my despatch. Moltke added that, much as he hated war, he did not see how Germany could avoid it next year, unless the great powers 'coalesced' to persuade France to reduce her armaments to a reasonable peace establishment.

Then Nothomb told me that Bismarck had sent Bülow to him with the following confidential message: 'Tell your King to get his army ready for defence, because Belgium may be invaded by France sooner than we expect.'

This message Nothomb writes to Brussels today. He is under the impression that in the event of war, Bismarck intends to occupy Belgium, as Frederick the Great occupied Saxony when he suspected Maria Theresa of wanting to take her revenge for the loss of Silesia. This is curious, and you will probably hear more about it from Brussels.

Lord Newton, *Lord Lyons: A Record of British Diplomacy*, Vol. II, p. 74.

(b)

On 6 May 1875, Lord Odo Russell reported that Count Schouvaloff, the Russian Ambassador in London, had just arrived at Berlin from St Petersburg.

The good news he brought respecting our relations with Russia filled me with delight after the dark allusions made to me here at court and by the Chancellor during the winter. As regards Germany and the war rumours, Count Schouvaloff gave me the most satisfactory and welcome news that the Emperor of Russia is coming to Berlin on Monday next, will insist on the maintenance of peace in Europe, even at the cost of a rupture with Germany, and that he can reckon on the support of Austria in doing so.

How Bismarck will meet the humiliating blow of being told by his allies, Russia and Austria, that he must keep the peace with France, when he has proclaimed to the world that France is ready to take her revenge, it is difficult to foretell. But we must not be surprised if it hastens on the outburst it is intended to prevent. I hope not, and do not expect it, but I shall not be surprised if it does, because Austria has really joined Russia. She has become an obstacle in the way of German development, which Bismarck will try to remove.

Lord Newton, *Lord Lyons: A Record of British Diplomacy*, Vol. II, p. 76.

(c) Lord Odo Russell to Lord Derby

Berlin, 12 November 1875

. . . The joint action of Russia and England last May, in the interest of peace, took him [Bismarck] by surprise, destroyed his fondest calculations, and left him isolated and disappointed to reflect on the possibility of a peace coalition against Germany, which he could not break up without the certainty of Russian neutrality or assistance. He feels that Gortchakoff has abandoned him for the time being, that he has lost the confidence of the Emperor Alexander, and that while they live, there is but little hope of a change of policy in Russia, favourable to his plans – viz. the breaking up of Austria and the neutralization of the minor German sovereignties.

Bismarck reckoned much on his friend Schouvaloff, but Schouvaloff turned traitor last May, and is less German in England than he was in Russia, which Bismarck cynically attribute[s] to the influence of wine and women. . . .

On the whole the present situation of affairs seems to me favourable to the maintenance of peace.

Of course we must be prepared for an occupation of some portions of European Turkey by Austria and Russia, but that need not necessarily lead to war.

I have also endeavoured to find out what the views of the National Party in regard to the east really are, and I find that the breaking up of European Turkey would be received with satisfaction, for the Turk has no friends in Germany. The German provinces of Austria are looked upon as the natural and inevitable inheritance, sooner or later, of the

German Empire, for which Austria might be compensated in Turkey, with or without Constantinople. Some people talk wildly of giving Constantinople to Greece, as less likely to be objected to by the western powers. But even Russia might take possession of Constantinople without objection on the part of Germany. Anything calculated to break the influence of France in the east, which is still thought to be too great, would be popular in Germany, and more especially if the interests of the Latin Church could be injured by it.

England may have Egypt if she likes. Germany will graciously not object.

Since May it has become manifest that Russia has the power to hamper the movements of Germany and arrest her progress effectually, and that Germany can undertake nothing new without the passive consent of Russia. This power must be so intolerable to Bismarck that he is sure to exercise all his skill in drawing Russia out of the combined arms of the great powers, back into his own exclusive embrace. . . .

Bismarck's endeavours last winter to make us suspicious of Russia, and vice versa, are now fully explained. His failure must add to the general irritation he suffers from.

Lord Newton, *Lord Lyons: A Record of British Diplomacy*, Vol. II, pp. 88 f.

7 The Nightmare of Coalitions, 1877

OTTO VON BISMARCK

This document, dictated by Bismarck on 15 June 1877, is the classic statement of the aims of Bismarckian diplomacy after the 1875 crisis.

A French newspaper said recently of me that I had 'le cauchemar des coalitions'; this kind of nightmare will be a very justified one for a German minister to have for a long time to come, if not indeed for ever. Coalitions against us could be formed on the basis of the western powers with the addition of Austria, or – perhaps more dangerous still – on a Russian–Austrian–French basis; a great intimacy between any two of the three last-named powers would give the third of them the means to exercise very effective pressure on us at any time. In view of these

the collapse of a giant empire but go on to conquer the conquerors. . . . One comes to the conviction that far greater things might be in the offing than those now in power could possibly suspect'. In 1923, in an amazing letter, he hailed Hitler as the messiah of Germany.

At the same time it is important to remember that, despite the acceptance of anti-Semitic ideas in Imperial Germany, Jews there were still very much better off than in the western areas of Russia, and that there was nothing in the Second Reich to compare with the pogroms of the East or the Dreyfus Affair in France. It took the violent social changes produced by the First World War, the inflation and the Great Depression to persuade a large number of Germans to accept the fanatical beliefs of Hitler.

1 Judaism in Music, 1850

RICHARD WAGNER

Wagner's essay on Judaism in Music *appeared in 1850, well before Bismarck unified Germany and immediately after the failure of the 1848 revolutions, in which Wagner himself had taken an active part in Dresden. The great composer's anti-Semitic outburst has been variously explained as the product of a personal feud with Meyerbeer and as a result of his own partly Jewish origin (according to Nietzsche, Wagner was the illegitimate son of the Jewish actor Ludwig Geyer). In its emphasis on the physical characteristics of Jewish people, however, it was by no means untypical of anti-Semitic sentiments widespread then and later.*

The Jew who, as we all know, claims to have a God all to himself, arrests our attention in ordinary life firstly by his exterior appearance. It matters not to which particular European nationality he may belong, the Jew's appearance strikes us as something so unpleasantly incongruous that, involuntarily, we wish to have nothing in common with him. Formerly no doubt this redounded to his misfortune, but nowadays we cannot fail to recognize it as a misfortune which quite permits of his still feeling very well; so much so, that, considering the measure of his success, his dissimilarity from us is even liable to be esteemed by himself as a distinction. We are not concerned with the moral side of this disagreeable play of nature but merely with the consideration of its relation to art; and, in this connection, must be mentioned the inconceivability of the Jew's exterior as a representative medium.

Thus, when plastic art wishes to represent the Jew, it generally draws its model from imagination; either discreetly ennobling or leaving out altogether those traits which characterize his presence in ordinary life. Never in his wanderings does he stray upon the theatrical stage; exceptions to this being so rare, both in point of number and in respect of the circumstances attending them, that they may be said to confirm the rule.

No character, whether antique or modern, hero or lover, can be even thought of as represented by a Jew without an instant consciousness on our part of the ludicrous inappropriateness of such a proceeding. This is extremely important; for, if we hold a man to be exteriorly disqualified by race for any artistic presentment whatever – that is to say, not merely for any one in particular but for all without exception – it follows that we should also regard him as unfit for any artistic pronouncement. . . .

The general circumstance that a Jew speaks his modern European language only as if acquired and not as if he were native to it shuts him out from all capability of full, independent and characteristic expression of his ideas. A language is not the work of one man, but its mode of expression and its development are the joint emanation of an ancient community; and only he whose life has been fostered within that community can expect to take part in its creations. But alone with his Jehovah stood the Jew outside all such, his race divided and bereft of native land, with all development denied to it; even its peculiar tongue – the Hebrew – being only sustained to it as a dead language.

Even the greatest genius has hitherto found it impossible to write genuine poetry in a foreign tongue. But in the position of a foreign tongue to the Jew has our entire European civilization remained. As in the formation of the one so in the development of the other he has borne no part, but, at the most, merely looked on, with feelings cold and even hostile, as is natural to a homeless unfortunate. In such language or in such art the Jew can naturally but echo and imitate, and is perforce debarred from fluent expression and pure creative work. . . .

But, if the defects of speech to which reference has been made practically withhold from the Jew the capacity for all artistic delivery of feeling through the medium of spoken words, it follows that, through the medium of song, such expression must be far more distinctly impossible. Song, for example, is but speech intensified or raised to the level of passion. If the Jew, in allowing himself a greater intensity of expression through the medium of speech, may make himself ridiculous, but cannot excite our sympathy in the least degree, he will, should he proceed to the height of song, become entirely unsupportable. In the latter, everything which had previously moved us unfavourably, whether relating to his speech or to his outward appearance, becomes intensified; and we are either driven from the scene or else chained to the spot by the utter absurdity of such a manifestation. In song the peculiarity of the Jewish nature which affects us so disagreeably is very naturally at its height, considering that song is the most vivid and unquestionably the truest expression of personal feeling; so that, to whatever branch of Art we may feel inclined to admit the Jews as capable, that of song, at all events, must to him, by a natural admisson be eternally denied.

Judaism in Music ('Das Judenthum in der Musik'), 1850, translated by Edwin Evans Snr., London, William Reeves, 83 Charing Cross Road, W.C., 1910, pp. 9–16.

2 Masculine and Feminine Races, 1868
OTTO VON BISMARCK

Bismarck was not a nationalist but a conservative statesman who was prepared to use nationalism if it served his purpose. However, he at times expressed himself in almost racialist terms, as in this conversation with the National Liberal Professor Bluntschli of 1868, in which Bismarck echoes the ideas of the French racialist thinker Count Gobineau.

Perhaps it will seem fantastic to you if I say that, as in nature itself, some nations are masculine and others feminine. The Teutons are so masculine that, taken individually, they are quite ungovernable. Each conducts his life as he pleases. But when they are rallied together they are irresistible, like a torrent which destroys everything in its path. Feminine, on the other hand, are the Slavs and the Celts. Of their own accord they can do nothing, they are not productive. The Russians can do nothing without the Germans. They cannot work but they are easy to lead. They have no power of resistance and they follow their leader. The Celts too are nothing but a passive mass. Not until the Teutons arrived on the scene and mixed with them did peoples capable of setting up States arise. Thus the English, the Spanish so long as they were led by Goths, and the French so long as the Frankish element was in the lead. The French Revolution has expelled the latter and so led to the domination of the Celtic element once more. That causes the French to tend to subordinate themselves to authority. The Westphalians and Swabians are pure Teutons and hardly mixed, and consequently it is difficult to accustom them to the idea of a state. But when they are gripped by a national idea and become wild, they will move mountains. But that seldom happens. As a rule every village and every peasant wants to be left to himself. Among the Prussians there is a strong mixture of Slavic and Teutonic elements. That is one main cause of their usefulness to the State. They have something of the subordinate character of the Slavs and yet something of the strength and manliness of the Teutons.

Die Gesammelten Werke. Otto Stollberg and Co, Verlag für Politik und Wirtschaft, Berlin, 1924, Vol. 7, No. 199, pp. 253 f.

3 Bismarck's Views on Anti-Semitism

HEINRICH VON POSCHINGER

He [Bismarck] did not see any way by which the aims of the anti-Semites might be realized. If one questioned them about the practical execution of their plans, they became like the Social Democrats; they were unable to propose anything that could be practically carried out; their recipes were not applicable to the organism of the State of today. Moreover, what could one do? Measures like Bartholomew's Eve or the Sicilian Vespers could hardly be proposed even by the anti-Semites themselves. Nor could the Jews be expelled without grave injury to the national welfare. Any measures by which the Jews would be excluded from judicial and other positions in the State would only increase the evil which the anti-Semites thought they had to do away with. For then the same Jewish intelligence, to which public careers would be closed, would embrace those fields in which the overweight of the Jew is already said by the anti-Semites to be intolerable, i.e. those of commerce.

The prince then stated his opinion that the Jewish movement sprang less from religious and social instincts than from economic reasons. He mentioned as a fact that the Jews are greatly superior to the other elements of the population in making money. Their superiority rests on qualities which, whether they are pleasing or not, cannot be removed by measures of State. The Jews, by reason of their natural dispositions, were generally more clever and skilful than Christians. They were also, at any rate so long as they had not made their fortunes, if perhaps not more industrious at least more frugal and saving than their Christian competitors. To this must be added the fact that the Jew would risk something more readily once in a way in order to gain a commercial advantage, and in applying his methods to gain his object, would also act more kind-heartedly than his Christian competitor. All this gives him an advantage in commerce which could not legally be taken away. Even the anti-Semites had up till then been unable to suggest anything which might paralyze this advantage and its effect on the economic life of the nation. Their proposals had hitherto been impracticable and no government would be found able to carry them out. It was also inadvisable for the State to put obstacles in the way of the pursuit of gain and fortune, for the other elements of the population would thereby suffer equally, and the national wealth would decrease.

Sidney Whitman, *Conversations with Bismarck*, collected by Heinrich von Poschinger. New York and London, 1900, pp. 164 ff.

4 An Anti-Semitic Cartoon

Der naie Kanzler!!

Ein freisinniger Traum.

A good example of the way in which the Conservatives after 1890 identified parliamentarianism and free trade with the Jews is provided by this cartoon of Eugen Richter, leader of one of the Left Liberal parties in the Reichstag.

Boetticher Papers, Bundesarchiv Koblenz.

Eugen

GOLDENE 110. G

NE 110.

Pour le Credit

MOSEL-FEBER

SPIRITUS OMNIBUS · VIRIS PAUPERIS

Alliance Israelit.

100,000 M.

Dem deutschen Michel gewidmet von

Peter Simpel.

5 Anti-Semitism at the Court of Wilhelm II, 1895

PHILIPP EULENBURG

*From 1886 to 1906, no one had a greater influence on Wilhelm II than Count,
later Prince, Philipp zu Eulenburg-Hertefeld, who in 1894 became Germany's
ambassador in Vienna. In 1882, Eulenberg had written the obituary on
Gobineau in the Wagnerian Bayreuther Blätter. In this letter of 1 September 1895 to the Kaiser, Eulenburg reveals the extent to which Wagner's
ideas had gained acceptance in the highest social circles in Germany.*

I beg Your Majesty most graciously to allow me to write a few words
today about the *Jewish question*, which is more acute in Austria than in
all other countries – probably because the carefree Austrian people have
laughingly allowed themselves to be cheated until they noticed one fine
day that the Jews had taken all their money. . . .

I shall write about Israel – in whose midst I spent four weeks in the
Hotel Bellevue in Vöslau – not in the form of a report but a character
sketch. I was the only Aryan in this guest-house which, like all the other
hotels in Vöslau (because of its nearness to Vienna and hence the possibility of doing business in the city) is occupied on all floors by the Cohn,
Levy, Aaron, etc. families.

The Jews are generous. This is one good quality they do possess;
though whether it is out of fear that they might get blows if they
refused to make the odd mild gesture is something I am not sure about –
but I would like to give full recognition to this good quality. There took
place, therefore, an amateur concert – in the best Vöslau tradition – in
which everyone who was musically gifted could take part. Since there
are *only* Jews in Vöslau at this time of the year, both the artists and the
spectators are *without exception* Jews. I receive an honorary invitation
and wish to show my goodwill. . . . At half past eight I arrive at the
door of the concert hall in the Hotel Bellevue and I am greeted with a
deep bow by a very aggressive-looking committee member in tails, his
Roman nose drooping slightly, his moustache brushed upwards, and
his red and white committee ribbon waving about next to his white
bow-tie. 'My name is Lieutenant Aaron, I have the honour, if you
please' – he says, and I am conducted through the over-full hall, which

39

is dripping with sweat, to my place of honour in the front, close to the small raised stage, just next to two smoking petroleum lamps. An enormous committee lady, from whose bare fat shoulders the sweat runs in streams into the abyss (there is supposed to be a dance after the concert – for anyone who still feels like it) curtsies smilingly and gracefully bows her huge little head in front of me until I sit down. This enormous matron was called Fräulein Lewyson. On my right was a very nice Frau Bach, to whom I was introduced by Lt Aaron, and on the left an old Jew who is accorded much honour; perhaps he has slaughtered and eaten Christian children, for two dozen long yellow fangs protrude from his horrible jaws and his woolly white goat hair grows to within a fraction of his red-rimmed eyes.

In front of us, between the stage and my chair, there is an excited and restless army of children; one can tell already whether they belong to the narrow-faced, bent-nosed or the broad-faced, blob-nosed variety of Jews.

An indescribable international gabble of Austrian–Bohemian–Hungarian German fills the air. A bell rings. Everyone falls silent, because the red curtain is supposed to go up – only it doesn't because it is pinned together in the middle. Much laughter in the hall. Committee member Lt Aaron removes the pin and, smiling sweetly, bows deeply. Great applause – he bows again and falls over a step in the stage exit. Another committee member helps him on to his cross legs.

I wish to add here that in the musical evening that now followed *each* of the participants, in understandable excitement, falls (or, if he is clever, only stumbles) over this step, and in fact twice, on coming on and again on leaving the stage.

There now appears, with a kind of somersault caused by stumbling, Fräulein Feiglstock. A young Jewish thing with nice colouring and pretty eyes, a blob-nose and an unspeakably huge, promising mouth which splits her face into two halves like a swallow's. But she has nice teeth, so that it was not really unpleasant to see into her intestines when she opened her mouth wide to reach the high notes. She sang a terribly disreputable song with the refrain 'in the night'. I asked my nice neighbour Frau Bach if she thought that little Miss Feiglstock understood what she was singing. She said 'Yes' – but regretted it very much. . . .

There then appeared – almost head-over-heels – an American Jew, Mr David, the quintessence of the broad-boned, blob-nosed Jew. Looking rough and evil and still young, he bowed in a way which might be common in America but has never been seen here before:

First both flat feet were turned to the right and he made short, vigorous nods of the head to the left. Then both flat feet to the left – and he bent the upper part of his body to the right. He had some sheet-music in his hand *behind which* he sang Rubenstein's 'Asra'. Only when he sang: 'and my tribe are the Asra who die when they love', in a dreadful nasal American, did he lower his music and there appeared, to the horror of the audience, such a ghastly face, such a terrible gaping mouth with hollow teeth, that one could believe not just that the Asra had died but that they had been strangled. Thank God this horrible person soon disappeared once more behind his music. My nice neighbour Frau Bach said only: 'the young man is not pretty'. I remarked that perhaps that was why he hid himself behind the music, but Frau Bach said 'Oh no'. . . .

Eulenburg to Wilhelm II, 1 September 1895. Bundesarchiv Koblenz, *Eulenburg Papers*, Vol. 37, pp. 591d–591l.

6 Kaiser Wilhelm II meets Houston Stewart Chamberlain, 1901

PHILIPP EULENBURG

It was Prince Eulenburg who, in 1901, brought Wilhelm II together with H. S. Chamberlain, the leading racialist thinker in Germany at the time and the son-in-law of Richard Wagner. Here Eulenburg describes the encounter.

When Kaiser Wilhelm read Houston Chamberlain's *The Foundations of the Nineteenth Century*, he became more fascinated than ever by the 'mission of Germandom' proclaimed by this spiritually so outstanding man. It also nourished, however, the belief which he had held since before his accession to the throne of a spiritual mission of the German Kaiser based on his personal power. . . .

At that time Chamberlain was in Vienna. I let him know that the Kaiser had gained such pleasure from his *Foundations* that I should be pleased to talk to him about it. He soon visited me and I then returned the visit.

It became evident that he was very interested in the person of the Kaiser and his furtherance of the German national cause, and he welcomed with enthusiasm my suggestion of a personal meeting between him and the Kaiser.

I decided to persuade Chamberlain to visit us at Liebenberg while the Kaiser was staying there, and as soon as the dates of the Kaiser's visit were fixed I wrote proposing this to him. The Kaiser was naturally delighted with my idea. . . .

28 October 1901. . . . While we were out walking the Reich Chancellor [Bülow] had arrived together with Chamberlain. . . . Chamberlain was greeted by the Kaiser in the library. It was a big moment for both men, and the Kaiser was moving in his gratitude to me for having arranged the encounter. . . .

After dinner the children again played some music. But not for as long as yesterday, for the Kaiser was burning with impatience to talk to his heart's content to the author of the *Foundations of the Nineteenth Century*, whom he rightly held in boundless esteem. Standing smoking apart from the other guests, he heard and saw nothing but Chamberlain all evening. . . .

29 October 1901. . . . The afternoon, spent in conversation around the fire in the library, was most interesting. . . . As usual, the Kaiser led the discussion – and in fact very well, as he speaks impressively and with confidence. . . . Chamberlain – with his fiery spirit and those eyes and looks which speak volumes – is the type of scholar who expresses himself better in writing than on the rostrum. If he was the most profound of the circle, the one whose remarks always touched on the inner and essential meaning of things, he was also the most taciturn. Bülow had little chance to shine as a conversationalist, though his extensive knowledge was adequately revealed. . . .

At about 5.30 we returned from our walk, and the children were asked to play music in the library. But then the Kaiser again went over to Chamberlain and Harnack and once more the 'mission of Germandom' was discussed from all possible angles, until I told the Kaiser that the clock had struck 6.30 and he had ordered dinner for 7 o'clock. . . .

The Kaiser could not thank me enough for the pleasure I had given him by arranging the meeting with Chamberlain. He stood completely under the spell of this man, whom he understood better than any of the other guests because of his thorough study of the *Foundations of the Nineteenth Century*. . . .

Philipp Fürst zu Eulenburg-Hertefeld, *Erlebnisse an deutschen und fremden Höfen*. Leipzig, 1934, Vol. 2, pp. 321–3, 329–30, 333, 335.

7 Chamberlain: The Mission of Germandom, 1901

HOUSTON STEWART CHAMBERLAIN

Chamberlain was an Englishman by birth. In this letter to Kaiser Wilhelm II, dated 15 November 1901, he explains why he chose to live in Germany.

. . . Your Majesty and all your subjects were born in a holy place; most of them, it is true, do not suspect it because they take it for granted – like the rays of the life-giving sun. I, however, had to follow a long and difficult path before I espied the holy shrine from afar, and it took many more years of hard work before I was able to ascend its steps. That is why I can only look back in horror at my past; because even though I had what one calls a happy childhood, for a man of my character there could be no true happiness outside of Germandom. I shudder to think how late in life I came into contact with the German language; I might easily not have learnt it at all. For it is my innermost belief – gained through years of study, gained in those sacred hours when the soul wrestles with divine wisdom, like Jacob with the angel – that the moral and spiritual salvation of mankind depends on things German. In that 'moral world order' of which Your Majesty often spoke at Liebenberg, the German element presently forms the crux, *le pivot central*. It is the German language which proves this incontestably; for science, philosophy and religion can today make no step forward except in the German language. From the existence of this language we learn something which is not always apparent in everyday life: that the highest qualities are united in this people, higher than may be found anywhere else.

Language and the national soul condition one another; each grows out of the other; so long as both remain alive and linked together, the plant will continue to flower. In the case of the Romance peoples, both are dead; in the case of the other Germans (I am thinking especially of England), the two have for some time been growing apart, with the result that the language is becoming ever more silent (that is, turning into a mere medium for communicating practical matters and losing all its inventiveness) and the soul is consequently shedding its flights and is simply dragging itself along on its belly like a worm. And since the German soul is bound indissolubly to the German language, it follows that the future progress of mankind is bound to a powerful Germany stretching far across the earth and preserving and imposing upon others the sacred heritage of its language. The actual *Realpolitik* of the German Reich, which surely cannot be really sober and matter of fact, therefore must be – at least in my view – quite distinct from the policies pursued by other countries. From the point of view of the moral world order, the Anglo-Saxon has forfeited his heritage – I speak not of today but look centuries ahead; the Russian is only the latest embodiment of the eternal empire of Tamburlain, and if one were to deprive it of its German dynasty, nothing would remain but a decaying *matière brute*; today God relies only on the Germans. That is the knowledge, the certain truth, which has filled my soul for years; in its service I have sacrificed my peace, for it I shall live and die. . . . My struggle – inspired not by hatred of Semites but by love of the Teutons – against the caustic poison of Judaism, my struggle against ultramontanism, against materialism; my attempt to transform the doctrine of transcendental knowledge from a possession of an academic caste into the possession of every educated German; my desire to divest religion of its Syrian–Egyptian rags, so as to enable the pure power of faith to unite us where the thoughtless repetition of slavish superstitions now only divides us; and later – if I live to see the day – the complete transformation of our conception of the life-problem so that our natural sciences will suddenly and for the first time find themselves in harmony with our German philosophy and religion, so giving us a true *Weltanschauung* at last . . . all this means for me fighting and creating in the service of Germandom. For verily, the issues at stake are of great import, and if the creator of the moral world order has chosen the Germans as his instruments, then they must submerge themselves completely in the pursuance of this God-given duty. And if 'things German' are, as I said above, the central pivot on which the future of man's spirit depends, then the present moment, the present century – and I mean it – is the central pivot of world history. The issue now is: to make or to mar.

There are times when history is, so to speak, woven ... according to a fairly well-established pattern; but then come times when the threads for a new tapestry must be introduced, when the nature of the cloth and the pattern to be woven have to be determined, and care taken to ensure a purposeful procedure. We find ourselves in such a time today. The creation of the German Reich was not a beginning but an end. Now there will either be a 'new course' (as Your Majesty recently remarked) or else nothing at all; and in the latter instance Germany will have failed and will move slowly towards its downfall, to be overtaken and drowned in the waves of a Yankee-ized Anglo-Saxondom and a tartarized Slavdom. This is the moment when the future is being decided. ...

On the other hand, how could a man like myself possibly study history without concluding that the future of the German cause is bound up with the Hohenzollern dynasty? How could one possibly observe the present political chaos of the Reich with its Reichstag without feeling that one's hopes could be based only on the dynasty? True, the entire German people with its incomparable language is the source of that strength without which the Hohenzollerns would themselves be nothing; but political salvation cannot be achieved by the people. In this extremely difficult world situation the House of Hohenzollern is the only trump card held by the German people. Only planned organization down to the minutest detail, and not – as with the Anglo-Saxons – the untrammelled liberty of the atomized individual, can help Germany to victory. Political freedom for the masses is a spent force; by using the principle of organization, however, Germany can achieve anything – anything! In this respect she has no equal. And at the head of this organization stands, as the foremost German of them all, the King of Prussia.

Briefe. München, 1928, Vol. II, pp. 137 ff.

8 The Struggle against Rome and Jerusalem, 1901

KAISER WILHELM II

The Kaiser replied to Chamberlain's letter on the last day of 1901.

My dear Mr Chamberlain,

Unhappily you are completely correct in saying at the start of your compelling and gripping letter that you assume I know nothing about the 'Upanishads' and other Indo-Aryan books, nor about the beautiful sayings of the wise men concerning rulers, which are contained therein. I openly admit my ignorance and beg for mercy! Here you have me at a disadvantage! But in the early 70s there was no one, certainly among my teachers, who had the slightest knowledge of such matters! ... We had to wade through 1000 pages of grammar, we applied the rules, and attacked everything from Phidias to Demosthenes, from Pericles to Alexander, and even our dear great Homer, with a magnifying glass and scalpel! And throughout all these hundreds of surgical operations which I had to carry out upon the products of the Hellenes so as to get a 'classical education', my heart rebelled and the lively feeling for harmony which I possess cried out: 'Surely this is not, this cannot be, what we need from Hellas for the advancement of Germandom'! - and this immediately after and still under the overpowering impression of the 1870 war, of the victories of my father and grandfather! They had forged the German Reich, and I felt instinctively that we boys needed another type of preparation if we were to continue the good work in the new Reich. Our severely depressed youth had need of a liberator like yourself! - someone who revealed the Indo-Aryan sources to us. But no one knew them!

And consequently all that massive primeval Aryan–Germanic feeling which lay slumbering within me had to fight its own way gradually to the fore. It came into open conflict with 'traditional wisdom', expressed itself frequently in a bizarre form, frequently without form at all, because it was more like a dark sentiment stirring in my subconscious and trying to break free. Then you come along – with one magic stroke you bring order into the confusion, light into the dark-

46

ness, aims for which we can strive and work, explanations for things which we sensed only darkly, paths which must be followed for the salvation of the Germans and thus for the salvation of mankind! You sing in high praise of things German and above all of our magnificent language and you cry out impressively to the Teuton: 'Forget your quarrels and pettiness; your task on earth is: to be God's instrument for the spreading of His culture, His teaching! Hence deepen, raise, cultivate your language and through it science, enlightenment and faith!' That was a liberation! So! And now you know, my dear Mr Chamberlain, what was going on in my mind when I felt your hand in mine!

Allow me to thank you for this precious jewel which you sent me in the form of a letter! Who am I, that you thank me? Surely only a poor child which tries to be a good instrument for our lord God up there. . . .

Truly, let us thank Him up there, that He still looks with such, such favour upon our Germans; for God sent your book to the German people and you personally to me, that is a firm belief which no one can destroy in one. You were chosen by Him to be my ally, and I shall thank Him eternally that He did so. For your powerful language grips people and forces them to think and naturally also to fight, to attack! What harm will it do! The German sleepy-head is waking up, and that is a good thing, then he will be on the look-out and will achieve something; and once he has begun to work he will achieve more than anyone else. His science in his own language is a gigantic weapon, and he must be reminded of this constantly! For 'Reason' – i.e. common sense – and 'Science' are our most dangerous weapons, especially in the fight against the deadly power of 'Ubiquitous' Rome. Once the teutonic Catholics have been led by you into the open conflict between Teutons and the Catholics, that is 'Romans', then they will be 'awakened' and will 'perceive' that which the father confessors are trying to hide from them – that they are being kept in degrading subjection to 'Rome' as an instrument against 'Germany'. Therefore 'Eritis sicut deus, scientes bonum et malum'. It is now possible to perceive a movement in this direction, and your book is being widely bought in such circles, praise God!

I first read your wonderful letter myself, and then I read it out to all the people gathered around my Christmas table. All ranks and generations listened in silence and were deeply moved. The Kaiserin sends you her sincere thanks and wishes!

And now I wish God's blessing and the grace of our Saviour upon my comrade-in-arms and ally in the struggle for the Teutons against

Rome, Jerusalem, etc. The feeling that we are fighting for an absolutely good, divine cause is our guarantee of victory! . . .

Your loyal and grateful friend,

Wilhelm II R

H. S. Chamberlain, *Briefe*, Vol. II, pp. 141 ff.

9 The Misunderstood Bismarck

HEINRICH CLASS

The journalist Maximilian Harden was a fervent Bismarckian, but as a Jew he was expelled from one Bismarckian society, as Heinrich Class, the leader of the Pan-German League, recounts.

Where Kollman [a Silesian industrialist] stood politically became obvious on entering his house. In the magnificent hall there was a first-rate bust of Bismarck, on the walls pictures of all sorts connected with Bismarck. An original Lenbach hung in his study. Bismarck was the hero of his life; whoever was against Bismarck was his enemy.

Kollmann's love for Bismarck led him to join the circle of Bismarck admirers who met each evening at Hiller's in the Unter den Linden. Maximilian Harden was one of its most celebrated members. When he mentioned this name I cried in shocked tones: 'What, you and this scoundrel!' He replied: 'Wait until you hear the rest'. And he went on:

'A few years after Bismarck's death we convened once more. As usual the whole conversation centred around Bismarck, and one outdid the other in recollections of the common hero. Harden sat opposite me and I noticed that throughout he was looking at us mockingly, as though he were making fun of us. Suddenly he interrupted one gentleman with the words: "You and your Bismarck! What's so good about him? It was I alone who made him great." Stunned silence. But I, who was at that time still a passionate sort of fellow, stood up, seized an empty Bordeaux bottle and shouted at him: "You damned Jewboy!" So doing I smashed the bottle over his head so hard that glass flew in all directions. Blood streamed from the Jew's head. My friends were afraid I'd broken his skull – but it wasn't so serious. I had only given him something to remember me by. A man of his kind trying to insult Bismarck.'

I asked whether the incident had had any sequel. He answered: 'None at all. The Jew undertook no action whatever against me. He never showed his face in our circle again after that. One more thing: I was not an anti-Semite till then. It was Harden who turned me into one.'

Wider den Strom. Leipzig, K. F. Koehler Verlag, 1932, pp. 228 f.

10 The Jewish Question, 1913
KONSTANTIN VON GEBSATTEL

After the Reichstag elections of January 1912, in which the Social Democrats gained one-third of the votes and one-quarter of the seats, a plan for a new constitution was drafted by a retired Bavarian general and sent to the Prussian Crown Prince in October 1913. Among its many reactionary proposals was one for changing the status of Jews.

I am not an anti-Semite. I know some Jews, particularly business people, whom I respect and admire. On the other hand one would be blinder than Hödur [the Nordic god of darkness] if one stubbornly refused to see that our entire life is dominated and endangered by the Jewish spirit: internal affairs by the press in Jewish hands, financial affairs by the great banks directed by Jews, legal affairs by the huge number of Jewish lawyers in the big cities, cultural affairs by the many Jewish university professors and the almost exclusively Jewish theatre directors and critics. The Jewish and Germanic spirits contradict each other like fire and water: the latter is deep, positive and idealistic, the former superficial, negative, destructively critical and materialistic. The danger threatening Germandom and thus also the German Reich is grave and immediate; the more dangerous because it is cleverly disguised and because the Jewish press has succeeded in persuading a large section of the nation that anyone who fights against the excesses of Judaism is backward and inferior. I, on the other hand, maintain that anyone who fails to take up this struggle even for one day is avoiding his urgent duty in a cowardly way. . . .

The Jews should be placed under the law pertaining to aliens and should remain the guests of the German people. Naturally they will be exempt from military service and will pay instead an army tax, which will perhaps be up to twice as high as the taxes paid by Germans. Obviously they will not be allowed to enter public service, to be judges, officials, university professors, lawyers, officers; they will, however, be allowed to become businessmen, directors of private banks, doctors. The acquisition of sizeable landed estates will also be forbidden to them, and here the borderline will have to be drawn very low. For quarrels among themselves one could perhaps give them their own courts, but for quarrels with Teutons, they will come before the normal courts, as in the case of criminal proceedings.

There is a danger that such laws might cause the Jews to emigrate to States where they hoped to receive equal treatment with Christians, or rather, where they hoped to seize the entire executive power for themselves. I am sincerely convinced that Sombart is wrong when he declares that the expulsion of the Jews was the reason for the economic collapse of States in the Middle Ages, and I would point there rather to the Germanic prophet Count Gobineau. That German commerce does not need the Jews is proven by the Fuggers, the Welsers and the Hanseatic League, none of which succumbed to Jewish influence. I also know of not one case where a Jew has achieved great things in industry. I do admit, however, that a total emigration of Jews would be undesirable, and that we should try to use their good qualities to our advantage. I also do not know whether the German Reich could withstand the great capital loss involved, which I estimate in milliards. It would, in any case, be a travesty of justice if we were to permit our guests to take with them the great riches which they have only gained by being more commercially-minded and unscrupulous than their hosts, so doing great damage to the nation's prosperity. Any Jew wishing to emigrate must therefore leave the major share of his property to the State. It will therefore be necessary when the state of siege is proclaimed, to close the borders and the banks until the Jewish fortune has been assessed.

A mixing of Jewish and Germanic races is not desirable, but cannot be prevented. Baptism must not, however, change the status of the Jew and the Jewess, nor of their children. . . . Not until there is not more than one-quarter of Jewish blood in the grandchildren should these be able to acquire the rights of the Teutons. . . .

As the Jews are only guests and not citizens, they should not be allowed to participate in the discussions about the constitution, the rights of the citizen, etc. They must therefore be prohibited from editing and writing for newspapers, on pain of severe punishment. They will only be allowed to publish a fixed number of Jewish newspapers, specifically marked as such, solely about Jewish matters and devoid of all opinion and comment on affairs of state. . . .

May the man come soon who will lead us along this path. . . .

Konstantin Freiherr von Gebsattel, 'Gedanken über einen notwendigen Fortschritt in der inneren Entwicklung Deutschlands', *Deutsches Zentralarchiv*, Potsdam, Alldeutscher Verband, 204.

11 Wilhelm II and the Jews, 1913

KAISER WILHELM II

The Crown Prince was enthusiastic about Gebsattel's plans, and sent them post-haste to the Chancellor. Bethmann Hollweg was firm in his rejection of any such schemes, and appealed to the Kaiser to keep his son under control. In writing to the Crown Prince, Wilhelm II also firmly rejected the core of the general's proposal, but on the Jewish question he was more ambivalent.

Completely childish are the ideas of the Bavarian reformer on the expulsion of the Jews from the Reich. They would take their enormous riches with them, and we would strike a blow against our national welfare and economy which would put us back 100 years, and at the same time leave the ranks of the cultured nations.

On the other hand, our aim must certainly be firmly to exclude Jewish influence from the army and administration, and restrict its power in all artistic and literary activity. As far as the Jewish-influenced press is concerned, I agree with you entirely: that is where Judaism has found its most dangerous battleground. To get this under control and to put a stop to its dirty search for scandal and libel is an extremely

important task. But it is a difficult one and can only be solved by preserving the freedom of the rest of the press. For this is useful and
indispensable in a modern State as a safety valve for all kinds of pains
and discomforts which would seek expression otherwise in more
dangerous ways.

Hartmut Pogge-von Strandmann, 'Staatsstreichpläne, Alldeutsche und
Bethmann Hollweg', *Die Erforderlichkeit des Unmöglichen*. Frankfurt
a.M., Europäische Verlagsanstalt, 1965, pp. 38 f.

12 Hitler, the True Awakener, 1923

HOUSTON STEWART CHAMBERLAIN

*In a remarkable letter of 7 October 1923, a month before Hitler's abortive
beer-hall putsch, Chamberlain recognised in Hitler the future saviour of
Germany.*

Most respected and dear Herr Hitler,
    You have every right not to expect this surprise attack, since you
have seen with your own eyes how difficult it is for me to speak. But I
cannot resist the urge to say a few words to you. I regard this as an
entirely unilateral act, however – i.e. I do not expect an answer from
you.
    I have been thinking why it should have been you of all people – you
who are so successful at awakening people from their sleep and slovenli-
ness – who recently gave me a longer and more refreshing sleep than I
have had since that fateful day in August 1914 when I was smitten with
this treacherous illness. Now I believe I understand that precisely this is
the essence of your being: the true awakener is simultaneously the
bestower of peace.
    You are not at all, as you were described to me, a fanatic. I would
rather describe you as the direct opposite of a fanatic. The fanatic makes
people into hotheads, you warm people's hearts. The fanatic wants to
talk people into something, you want to convince them, only to convince them – and that is why you succeed. In fact, I would also describe

you as the opposite of a politician – in the ordinary sense of the word – for the root of all politics is membership of a party, whereas in your case all parties disappear, devoured by the heat of your love for the Fatherland. It was, in my opinion, the misfortune of our great Bismarck, that he . . . became a little too involved in politics. May you be spared this lot! . . .

I constantly ask myself whether the lack of political instinct of which the German is so widely accused may not be a symptom of a much deeper talent for State-building. At any rate the German's organizational talent is unsurpassed (see Kiaochow!) and his scientific ability is second to none: it is on this that I have based my hopes in my essay *Political Ideals*. It should be the ideal of politics to have *none*. But this non-politics would have to be frankly admitted and forced upon the world through the exercise of power. Nothing will be achieved so long as the parliamentary system obtains; for this the Germans have, God knows, not a spark of talent! I regard its continued existence as the greatest misfortune, it can lead only again and again into the mire and ruin all plans for restoring the health and the prestige of the Fatherland.

However, this is a digression, for I only wanted to speak of you. That you gave me peace is connected very much with your eyes and the motions of your hands. Your eyes seize people and hold them fast, as if with hands, and you have the singular habit of addressing yourself to one particular member of your audience at any one moment – I noticed this to be completely characteristic. As for your hands, they are so expressive in their movements that they are like eyes in this respect. It is hardly surprising that a man like that can give peace to a poor suffering spirit!

Especially when he is dedicated to the service of the Fatherland.

My faith in Germandom has not wavered for a moment, though my hopes were – I admit it – at a low ebb. With one blow you have transformed the state of my soul. That Germany, in the hour of her greatest need, brings forth a Hitler – that is proof of her vitality . . . that the magnificent Ludendorff openly supports you and your movement: What wonderful confirmation!

I could go untroubled to sleep, and there was no need for me to have woken up. May God protect you!

Briefe, Vol. II, pp. 124–6.

III
Germany and the First World War

Fritz Fischer's study of German aims in the First World War, which is now available in English translation, has revolutionized our interpretation not only of the war itself, but of the course of German history as well. Fischer's conclusions on Germany's war aims were so well documented that they have now been almost wholly accepted, though there is still some dispute about Chancellor Bethmann Hollweg's rôle in their formulation. The real controversy turned on the question of Germany's responsibility for causing the war. At first, Fischer had asserted only that Berlin had 'risked' the outbreak of a major war by supporting and encouraging Austria-Hungary to attack Serbia; later he moved to the position of regarding Germany as deliberately seeking a conflict with France and Russia while there still seemed to be a chance of achieving 'world power' — a view he will try to substantiate in his new book *Krieg der Illusionen* (Düsseldorf, 1969). After the initial, overwhelmingly hostile reaction, most German historians now accept the first of these positions, and many come close to accepting the second. Among the many factors contributing to this remarkable transformation, the discovery of new evidence – some of which is printed below – has been the most decisive. It is now clear, as Ludwig Dehio urged many years ago, that the two world wars were 'like two consecutive acts of the same drama', even though Hitler's war shows a 'daemonic' character absent from the Kaiser's.

1 Napoleonic Supremacy, 1892

KAISER WILHELM II

During a conversation on board the royal yacht in July 1892, the Kaiser and Eulenburg spoke as follows:

THE KAISER: I hope Europe will gradually come to realize the fundamental principle of my policy: *leadership* in the peaceful sense – a sort of Napoleonic supremacy – a policy which gave expression to its ideas by force of arms – in the peaceful sense. I am of the opinion that it is already a success that I, having come to govern at so early an age, stand at the head of *German* armed might yet have left my sword in its scabbard and have given up Bismarck's policy of eternally causing disruption to replace it with a peaceful foreign situation such as we have not known for many years. Slowly people will come to realize this. . . .

THE KAISER: I have my good reasons for being friendly to the Poles. After I had already discovered secretly that the mood in Posen and Russian Poland had changed completely in my favour, my old childhood and student friend, the American Bigelow, has made remarkable revelations to me from Warsaw. . . . He discovered to his surprise, that the whole interest, the whole hope of the Poles is now directed towards me and that every meeting begins with a toast to me. They are completely filled with the hope of being liberated from the Russian yoke, and in the event of a war with Russia the whole of Poland would revolt and come over to my side with the express intention of being annexed by me.

EULENBURG: But with the hidden thought of attaining the creation of a Polish Empire.

THE KAISER: No. They have given that up. The educated elements are aware of their own weakness. They want to come under Prussia. . . . In case of need, we could make Poland into an Imperial Territory. Alsace and Lorraine have proved the value of such an arrangement. I have *not* imparted Bigelow's information to the Foreign Office. There they would treat the Polish question to a certain extent as a political one – and I regard it for the time being purely from the *military* point of view. It is of the greatest advantage to our General Staff and the mobilization of our army to have Poland on our side. To ascertain whether Bigelow's information is correct, an officer of the General Staff has been sent secretly to Poland. Using Bigelow's contacts and with the help of the inhabitants, this man has been able to make incredible 'studies' – *of the greatest importance* for our mobilization. Everything that Bigelow wrote has been confirmed to the letter.

EULENBURG: If I, in spite of all this, still maintain my belief that the Poles continue to hope for independence and . . . wish to use Your Majesty only as a step towards independence, I by no means wish to belittle the value of Bigelow's information.

THE KAISER: That is *cura posterior*, anyway. For the *present*, *I* am their aim, and we ought not to forget it.

J. C. G. Röhl, 'A Document of 1892 on Germany, Prussia and Poland', *The Historical Journal*, VII, I, 1964, pp. 144 and 147.

2 Germany's Future Policy, 1896
ADMIRAL GEORG VON MÜLLER

In 1896, Admiral von Müller drafted a memorandum for the Kaiser's brother on what he thought Germany's aims in coming decades should be.

World history is now dominated by the economic struggle. This struggle has raged over the whole globe but most strongly in Europe, where its nature is governed by the fact that central Europe (*Mitteleuropa*) is getting too small and that the free expansion of the peoples who live here is restricted as a result of the present distribution of the inhabitable parts of the earth and above all as a result of the world domination of England. These countries are threatened with further restrictions both in trading activity and in the opportunity of accommodating their surplus population in their own colonies, so to make use of them in a national way. The war which could – and many say must – result from this situation of conflict would according to the generally accepted opinion in our country have the aim of breaking England's world domination in order to lay free the necessary colonial possessions for the central European states who need to expand.

These states are the German Reich, Austria-Hungary and Italy. The Scandinavian countries and Switzerland could with some justice also be included. But Germany stands far ahead in the need and indeed the right to expand – a right which is surely established by what she has already achieved in the field of world trade.

It is of course possible that her partners in the Triple Alliance, or at least Austria-Hungary, will stand at her side in this great battle for economic survival. But they and the German Reich would on no account be anything like strong enough to break England's world domination. France and Russia would also have to be won over. In France we would gain a considerable increase in naval power; and in Russia an ally who would be able to attack the British empire on land.

Let us now suppose that this chequered coalition really did succeed in destroying the British world empire: what would we have gained? The larger British colonies inhabited by Europeans – the autonomous colonies – would obviously become republics. Canada might even join the United States of North America – to strengthen which would hardly be in our interest.

Russia would naturally take India and therewith the lion's share of the spoils. Furthermore she would gain freedom of action in the Orient and China. France would take the English Channel Islands, would enlarge her tropical colonies in Africa and the West Indies and perhaps even Egypt might fall into her hands. For the other States in the coalition, and therefore also for Germany, the harvest – distributed according to the war effort as measured in naval strength – would naturally be less plentiful. It would be rash of us to expect much more than the enlargement of German East Africa.

And what would Germany have gained in respect of the general situation of world trade? The former British colonies would still wish to make themselves economically independent of Europe as at present, and those areas of the British Empire which would have fallen to Russia, France and the United States would be monopolitically exploited by the new motherland(s) at least as ruthlessly as they have ever been by England.

But the worst result of the great war would be the terrifying increase in Russia's strength. It is possible that for a short time our generation might be delighted at the downfall (*Untergang*) of British world power, but the next generation at the latest would have to suffer because we permitted Russia's power to grow to the skies – because we helped this already almost overpowerful State to free itself from its only serious rival in the struggle for world domination. And quite apart from that it would be a world-historical sin, a crime against general cultural progress, to deliver India into Russia's hands.

No, if that were the price then we would rather not become a colonial power at all. But might it not be possible to become a colonial power, and indeed one which would be economically and militarily stronger than would ever be possible as a result of an anti-English coalition, by allying *with* England?

England has at least as much if not actually more interest in keeping Russia down as we ourselves. If we support her in this task then perhaps we could count on England's support in the acquisition of territory outside Europe. It is a happy coincidence that this State could also be our natural ally because we are both of the same race. With England and ourselves fighting on the same side in this way, the economic struggle would acquire an idealistic element, i.e. the preservation of the Germanic race against the Slav and Romance peoples. . . .

Now we cannot expect a people so boundlessly common-sensical as the English to allow us to share in its world power domination simply because we are related to them. But we have, as we have seen, very important common interests which would surely provide the foundation for an arrangement whereby England would grant us benevolent freedom of action outside Europe or even support us directly in transforming spheres of interest into possessions or in granting Germany the areas she needs for expansion whenever foreign empires collapse. Naturally such an arrangement would have to be based on the principle of reciprocity. This might lead to England's being able to extend her world domination more swiftly, thanks to her much more powerful armaments, than we could expand ourselves, but even such a stronger Great Britain could never become as dangerous for us as a stronger Russia would be.

Here the objection might be raised that the end product of all this would be two Germanic world empires which would sooner or later but with absolute inevitability have to go to war to decide which of the two should dominate. And with England's great advantage as a sea power – and this is what really counts here – the odds would not be in Germany's favour. Well, all this is still a very long way off, and we ought surely not to exclude the possibility that two so-to-speak satiated colonial powers within each of which production would be roughly balanced against consumption could co-exist peaceably and use any surplus political power to further the struggle for the predomination of the

Germanic race. Besides, it is not at all certain that the British world empire would be the stronger of the two Germanic States, for the lead which Great Britain now has over us means that she will be faced correspondingly sooner with the natural tendency for colonies to break away to form independent States.

General von Caprivi [Bismarck's successor as Chancellor, 1890–94] believed that Germany had no chance at all of becoming a world power, and consequently his policy was designed only to maintain [Germany's] position on the European continent. He was therefore acting quite logically in working at home for the strengthening of the army, limiting the navy to the rôle of defending the coastline ... and seeking good relations with England as the natural ally against Russia, the country which threatened Germany's position in Europe.

Caprivi's policy, now so widely ridiculed, would have been brilliantly vindicated by history if the German people were not coming to accept an entirely different opinion of their ability and duty to expand than that expressed in our naval and colonial development so far.

Here, too, our motto must be all or nothing. *Either* we harness the total strength of the nation, ruthlessly, even if it means accepting the risk of a major war, *or* we limit ourselves to continental power alone. The middle way of contenting ourselves with a few left-over pieces of East Africa and the South Sea Islands without any or at most an extremely limited suitability for settlement by Germans; of maintaining a fleet too strong for the mere defence of our coastline yet too weak for the pursuance of *Weltpolitik* – all this implies a dispersal of our strength and a squandering of personal and material wealth which Caprivi's policy logically wished to see diverted to the army.

Will this policy turn out to have been right? We hope not. It would admittedly bring the present nation comfortable days without serious conflicts and excitements, but as soon as our exports began noticeably to decline the artificial economic edifice would start to crumble and existence therein would become very unpleasant indeed.

Now, the Caprivi policy has been officially abandoned, and the new Reich Government will hesitantly put to the nation the question – in the form of the new Navy Bill – whether the other policy, *Weltpolitik*, really can be adopted. Let us hope that this question receives an enthusiastic 'Yes' for an answer, but also that then a change comes over our external relations in favour of an understanding with England, beside which there is still a lot of room on this earth which is empty or could be made empty and against whose goodwill even a quite different naval development from the one that now appears to be envisaged would not be sufficient to pursue *Weltpolitik*, in spite of Russia's friendship.

W. Görlitz (ed.), *Der Kaiser.* Göttingen, Musterschmidt, 1965, pp. 36–41.

3 The Aims of German Policy, 1907

SIR EYRE CROWE

Crowe was the senior clerk in the Western Department of the British Foreign Office from 1906 to 1912. His views were strongly anti-German, but recent research has shown them to be fairly representative of opinion within the Foreign Office in the pre-war years. Crowe was, in fact, well-placed to assess German policy. He was born and educated in Germany, both his mother and his wife were German, and Admiral von Holtzendorff, Commander of the German Fleet until 1913, was his uncle.

With the events of 1871 the spirit of Prussia passed into the new Germany. In no other country is there a conviction so deeply rooted in the very body and soul of all classes of the population that the preservation of national rights and the realization of national ideals rest absolutely on the readiness of every citizen in the last resort to stake himself and his State on their assertion and vindication. With 'blood and iron' Prussia had forged her position in the councils of the great powers of Europe. In due course it came to pass that, with the impetus given to every branch of national activity by the newly-won unity and more especially by the growing development of oversea trade flowing in ever-increasing volume through the now Imperial ports of the formerly 'independent' but politically insignificant Hanse towns, the young empire found opened to its energy a whole world outside Europe, of which it had previously hardly had the opportunity to become more than dimly conscious. Sailing across the ocean in German ships, German merchants began for the first time to divine the true position of countries such as England, the United States, France and even the Netherlands, whose political influence extends to distant seas and continents. The colonies and foreign possessions of England more especially were seen to give to that country a recognized and enviable status in a world where the name of Germany, if mentioned at all, excited no particular interest. The effect of this discovery upon the German mind was curious and instructive. Here was a vast province of human activity to which the mere title and rank of a European great power were not in themselves a sufficient passport. Here in a field of portentous magnitude, dwarfing altogether the proportions of European countries, others, who had been perhaps rather looked down upon as comparatively smaller folk, were at home and commanded, while Germany was at best received but as an honoured guest. Here was distinct inequality, with a heavy bias in favour of the maritime and colonizing powers.

Such a state of things was not welcome to German patriotic pride. Germany had won her place as one of the leading, if not, in fact, the foremost power on the European continent. But over and beyond the European great powers there seemed to stand the 'world powers'. It was at once clear that Germany must become a 'world power'. The evolution of this idea and its translation into practical politics followed with singular consistency the line of thought that had inspired the Prussian kings in their efforts to make Prussia great. 'If Prussia', said Frederick the Great, 'is to count for something in the councils of Europe, she must be made a great power.' And the echo: 'If Germany wants to have a voice in the affairs of the larger oceanic world she must be made a "world power".' 'I want more territory,' said Prussia. 'Germany must have colonies,' says the new world-policy. And colonies were accordingly established, in such spots as were found to be still unappropriated, or out of which others could be pushed by the vigorous assertion of a German demand for 'a place in the sun'. On the whole, however, the 'Colonies' have proved assets of somewhat doubtful value.

Meanwhile the dream of a colonial empire had taken deep hold on the German imagination. Emperor, statesmen, journalists, geographers, economists, commercial and shipping houses and the whole mass of educated and uneducated public opinion continue with one voice to declare: We *must* have real colonies, where German emigrants can settle and spread the national ideals of the Fatherland and we *must* have a fleet and coaling stations to keep together the colonies which we are bound to acquire. . . .

No one who has a knowledge of German political thought and who enjoys the confidence of German friends speaking their minds openly and freely, can deny that these are the ideas which are proclaimed on the housetops and that inability to sympathize with them is regarded in Germany as the mark of the prejudiced foreigner who cannot enter into the real feelings of Germans. Nor is it amiss to refer in this connection to the series of Imperial apophthegms, which have from time to time served to crystallize the prevailing German sentiments and some of which deserve quotation: 'Our future lies on the water.' 'The trident must be in our hand.' 'Germany must re-enter into her heritage of maritime dominion once unchallenged in the hands of the old Hansa.' 'No question of world politics must be settled without the consent of the German Emperor.' 'The Emperor of the Atlantic greets the Emperor of the Pacific,' etc.

The significance of these individual utterances may easily be exaggerated. Taken together, their cumulative effect is to confirm the impression that Germany distinctly aims at playing on the world's political stage a much larger and much more dominant part than she finds allotted to herself under the present distribution of material power....

If it be considered necessary to formulate and accept a theory that will fit all the ascertained facts of German foreign policy the choice must lie between the two hypotheses here presented:

Either Germany is definitely aiming at a general political hegemony and maritime ascendency, threatening the independence of her neighbours and ultimately the existence of England;

Or Germany, free from any such clear-cut ambition and thinking for the present merely of using her legitimate position and influence as one of the leading powers in the council of nations, is seeking to promote her foreign commerce, spread the benefits of German culture, extend the scope of her national energies and create fresh German interests all over the world wherever and whenever a peaceful opportunity offers, leaving it to an uncertain future to decide whether the occurrence of great changes in the world may not some day assign to Germany a larger share of direct political action over regions not now a part of her dominions without that violation of the established rights of other countries which would be involved in any such action under existing political conditions.

In either case Germany would clearly be wise to build as powerful a navy as she can afford.

The above alternatives seem to exhaust the possibilities of explaining the given facts. The choice offered is a narrow one, nor easy to make with any close approach to certainty. It will, however, be seen, on reflection, that there is no actual necessity for a British Government to determine definitely which of the two theories of German policy it will accept. For it is clear that the second scheme (of semi-independent evolution, not entirely unaided by statecraft) may at any stage merge into the first, or conscious-design scheme. Moreover, if ever the evolution scheme should come to be realized, the position thereby accruing to Germany would obviously constitute as formidable a menace to the rest of the world as would be presented by any deliberate conquest of a similar position by 'malice aforethought'.

It appears, then, that element of danger present as a visible factor in one case, also enters, though under some disguise, into the second; and against such danger, whether actual or contingent, the same general line of conduct seems prescribed.

G. P. Gooch and H. Temperley, *British Documents on the Origins of the War*, Vol. III, Appendix A. H.M.S.O.

4 The Approach of War, 1913

J. A. CRAMB

If Sir Eyre Crowe could be suspected of anti-German prejudice, this is impossible in the case of another English observer, Professor J. A. Cramb. He too had studied at a German university and kept in closest touch with developments in Germany until his death in October 1913. Six months before he died, Cramb gave four lectures in London on 'Germany and England' in which, while expressing his profound admiration for German culture, he prophesied the imminent approach of war.

In regard to Germany we are confronted by certain circumstances that indisputably merit our consideration here in England. There is, for instance, the annual appearance in Germany of very nearly seven hundred books dealing with war as a science. This points, at once, to an extreme preoccupation in that nation with the idea of war. I doubt whether twenty books a year on the art of war appear in this country, and whether their circulation, when they do appear, is much more than twenty!

There is, again, the German way of regarding war. What is the attitude of mind towards war of Treitschke, for example, a man whose spirit still controls German youth, German patriotism, a man who has a power in Germany, as a thinker and as a writer, that you might compare to the power exercised by Carlyle and by Macaulay put together in this country? To him the army is simply the natural expression of the vital forces of the nation; and just as those vital forces of the nation increase so shall the German army and the German navy increase. A nation's military efficiency is the exact coefficient of a nation's idealism. That is Treitschke's solution of the matter. His answer to all our talk about the limitation of armaments is: Germany shall increase to the utmost of her power, irrespective of any proposals made to her by England or by Russia, or by any other State upon this earth. And I confess it is a magnificent and a manly answer, an answer worthy of a man whose spirit of sincerity, of regard for the reality of things, is as great as Carlyle's. . . .

That is the spirit in which war is regarded in contemporary Germany. And I am not the least astonished that when we send over from England an itinerant preacher of universal peace to explain to Germany, 'For the love of God, don't make war upon England; for it won't pay you' – I am not the least astonished that in a mass meeting of two thousand students at the University of Göttingen this itinerant preacher and all his works were set aside. How can we wonder at it? . . .

I have lived among Germans and know something of the temper of Germany's manhood and of her youth. I have read much in her history and in her literature. I have been impressed, as with the motion of tides and of great rivers, by the majesty of that movement by which, from the days of the Saxon and the Hohenstaufen Emperors, through centuries of feudal anarchy and disintegration made still more disintegrated by the convulsive forces of the fiercest religious strife, she has attained to her position today; and with the best will in the world I can see no issue to the present collision of ideals but a tragic issue. England, indeed, desires peace; England, indeed, it is certain, will never make war upon Germany; but how is the youth of Germany, the youth of that nation great in arts as in war, to acquiesce in the world-predominance of England? With what thoughts are they to read the history and the literature of their country? If, from love of peace or dread of war, Germany submits, it would seem as if her great soldiers had fought in vain, as if the long roll of her battles had passed like an empty sound, as if the Great Elector and Frederick, Stein and Scharnhorst and Bismarck had schemed in vain, as if her thinkers had thought their thoughts and her poets had dreamed their dreams not less in vain. But if, on the other hand, Germany has not declined from her ancient valour the issue is certain, and a speedy issue.

It is war.

J. A. Cramb, *Germany and England*. John Murray, June 1914, pp. 64–6 and 131–2.

5 World Power or Downfall, 1912

FRIEDRICH VON BERNHARDI

General Friedrich von Bernhardi's sensational book Germany and the Next War *appeared in 1912 and became an immediate best-seller. Most German historians firmly deny that the views held by Bernhardi were representative of official German policy. Professor Fritz Fischer, on the other hand, asserts that they 'epitomized the intentions of official Germany with great precision'.*

Under these conditions the position of Germany is extraordinarily difficult. We not only require for the full material development of our nation, on a scale corresponding to its intellectual importance, an extended political basis, but . . . we are compelled to obtain space for our increasing population and markets for our growing industries. But at every step which we take in this direction England will resolutely oppose us. English policy may not yet have made the definite decision to attack us; but it doubtless wishes, by all and every means, even the most extreme, to hinder every further expansion of German international influence and of German maritime power. The recognized political aims of England and the attitude of the English Government leave no doubt on this point. But if we were involved in a struggle with England, we can be quite sure that France would not neglect the opportunity of attacking our flank. Italy, with her extensive coast-line, even if still a member of the Triple Alliance, will have to devote large forces to the defence of the coast to keep off the attacks of the Anglo-French Mediterranean Fleet, and would thus be only able to employ weaker forces against France. Austria would be paralyzed by Russia; against the latter we should have to leave forces in the east. We would thus have to fight out the struggle against France and England practically alone with a part of our army, perhaps with some support from Italy. It is in this double menace by sea and on the mainland of Europe that the grave danger of our political position lies, since all freedom of action is taken from us and all expansion barred.

Since the struggle is, as appears on a thorough investigation of the international question, necessary and inevitable, we must fight it out, cost what it may. Indeed, we are carrying it on at the present moment, though not with drawn swords, and only by peaceful means so far. On the one hand it is being waged by the competition in trade, industries and warlike preparations; on the other hand, by diplomatic methods with which the rival States are fighting each other in every region where their interests clash.

With these methods it has been possible to maintain peace hitherto, but not without considerable loss of power and prestige. This apparently peaceful state of things must not deceive us, we are facing a hidden, but none the less formidable, crisis – perhaps the most momentous crisis in the history of the German nation.

We have fought in the last great wars for our national union and our position among the powers of Europe; we now must decide whether we wish to develop into and maintain a world empire, and procure for German spirit and German ideas that fit recognition which has been hitherto withheld from them.

Have we the energy to aspire to that great goal? Are we prepared to make the sacrifices which such an effort will doubtless cost us? or are we willing to recoil before the hostile forces, and sink step by step lower in our economic, political and national importance? That is what is involved in our decision. . . .

We must make it quite clear to ourselves that there can be no standing still, no being satisfied for us, but only progress or retrogression, and that it is tantamount to retrogression when we are contented with our present place among the nations of Europe, while all our rivals are straining with desperate energy, even at the cost of our rights, to extend their power. The process of our decay would set in gradually and advance slowly so long as the struggle against us was waged with peaceful weapons; the living generation would, perhaps, be able to continue to exist in peace and comfort. But should a war be forced upon us by stronger enemies under conditions unfavourable to us, then, if our arms met with disaster, our political downfall would not be delayed, and we should rapidly sink down. The future of German nationality would be sacrificed, an independent German civilization would not long exist, and the blessings for which German blood has flowed in streams – spiritual and moral liberty, and the profound and lofty aspirations of German thought – would for long ages be lost to mankind.

If, as is right, we do not wish to assume the responsibility for such a catastrophe, we must have the courage to strive with every means to attain that increase of power which we are entitled to claim, even at the risk of a war with numerically superior foes.

Under the present conditions it is out of the question to attempt this by acquiring territory in Europe. The region in the east, where German colonists once settled, is lost to us, and could only be recovered from Russia by a long and victorious war, and would then be a perpetual incitement to renewed wars. So, again, the re-annexation of the former South Prussia, which was united to Prussia on the second partition of Poland, would be a serious undertaking, on account of the Polish population.

Under these circumstances we must clearly try to strengthen our political power in other ways.

In the first place, our political position would be considerably con-solidated if we could finally get rid of the standing danger that France will attack us on a favourable occasion, so soon as we find ourselves involved in complications elsewhere. In one way or another we must square our account with France if we wish for a free hand in our inter-national policy. This is the first and foremost condition of a sound German policy, and since the hostility of France once for all cannot be removed by peaceful overtures, the matter must be settled by force of arms. France must be so completely crushed that she can never again come across our path.

Friedrich von Bernhardi, *Germany and the Next War*. Edward Arnold, 1914, pp. 103–6.

6 War in Eighteen Months, 1912

ADMIRAL GEORG VON MÜLLER

On 8 December 1912, a meeting took place at the New Palace in Potsdam at which the Kaiser discussed the developing situation in the Balkans with his top military and naval advisers, and in doing so almost uncannily predicted the sequence of events which actually occurred some eighteen months later, in July 1914. The meeting was recorded by Admiral von Müller, since 1906 head of the Kaiser's Naval Cabinet.

8 December 1912

Sunday. Called to His Majesty at 11 a.m. with Tirpitz, Heeringen (Vice-Admiral) and General von Moltke. H.M. speaks to a telegraphic report of the ambassador in London, Prince Lichnowsky, concerning the political situation. Haldane, speaking for Grey, has told Lichnowsky that England, if we attacked France, would unconditionally spring to France's aid, for England could not allow the balance of power in Europe to be disturbed. H.M. greeted this information as a desirable clarification of the situation for the benefit of those who had felt sure of England as a result of the recent friendliness of the press.

H.M. envisaged the following:

Austria must deal energetically with the foreign Slavs (the Serbs), otherwise she will lose control of the Slavs in the Austro-Hungarian monarchy. If Russia supports the Serbs, which she evidently does (Sasonoff's declaration that Russia will immediately move into Galicia if Austria moves into Serbia) then war would be unavoidable for us too. We could hope, however, to have Bulgaria and Rumania and also Albania, and perhaps also Turkey on our side. An offer of alliance by Bulgaria has already been sent to Turkey. We have exerted great pressure on the Turks. Recently H.M. has also pressed the Crown Prince of Rumania, who was passing through on his way back from Brussels, to come to an understanding with Bulgaria. If these powers join Austria then we shall be free to fight the war with full fury against France. The fleet must naturally prepare itself for the war against England. The possibility mentioned by the Chief of the Admiralty Staff in his last audience of a war with Russia alone cannot now, after Haldane's state-ment, be taken into account. Therefore immediate submarine warfare against English troop transports in the Scheldt or by Dunkirk, mine warfare in the Thames. To Tirpitz: speedy build-up of U-boats, etc. Recommendation of a conference of all interested naval authorities.

General von Moltke: 'I believe a war is unavoidable. But we ought to do more through the press to prepare the popularity of a war against Russia, as suggested in the Kaiser's discussion.'

H.M. supported this and told the State Secretary [Tirpitz] to use his press contacts, too, to work in this direction. T[irpitz] made the observation that the navy would prefer to see the postponement of the great fight for one-and-a-half years. Moltke says the navy would not be ready even then and the army would get into an increasingly unfavourable position, for the enemies were arming more strongly than we, as we were very short of money.

That was the end of the conference. The result amounted to almost nothing.

The Chief of the Great General Staff says: War the sooner the better, but he does not draw the logical conclusion from this, which is: To present Russia or France or both with an ultimatum which would un-leash the war with right on our side.

In the afternoon I wrote to the Reich Chancellor about the influenc-ing of the press.

J. C. G. Röhl, 'Admiral von Müller and the Approach of War', *The Historical Journal*, XII, 4 (1969), pp. 661 f.

7 The Army demands a Preventive War, 1914

GOTTLIEB VON JAGOW

One of the most interesting documents to come to light in the wake of the renewed controversy on Germany's policy in 1914 is the following record of a conversation between the German Foreign Secretary, von Jagow, and the Chief of the General Staff, von Moltke. The report was evidently written from memory after Germany's defeat, so that Jagow's arguments against preventive war should perhaps be treated with caution.

On 20 May and 3 June 1914 our Majesties gave lunches in the New Palace in Potsdam in honour of the birthdays of the Emperor of Russia and the King of England . . . to which the respective ambassadors – and therefore I too as State Secretary of the F.O. – were invited. On one of these occasions – I cannot remember whether it was the 20. 5. or the 6. 6. (*sic*) – the Chief of the General Staff, von Moltke, who was also present, said that he would like to discuss some matters with me, and asked whether I could not ride with him in his automobile on the return journey to Berlin. I accepted the invitation.

On the way Moltke described to me his opinion of our military situation. The prospects of the future oppressed him heavily. In two–three years Russia would have completed her armaments. The military superiority of our enemies would then be so great that he did not know how we could overcome them. Today we would still be a match for them. In his opinion there was no alternative to making preventive war in order to defeat the enemy while we still had a chance of victory. The Chief of General Staff therefore proposed that I should conduct a policy with the aim of provoking a war in the near future.

Moltke was not a man who lusted after the laurels of war. In our first conversation, at the beginning of the year 1913, I had been able to observe that he regarded the possibility of war with great gravity but without desiring a conflict. His present opinion was therefore all the more thought-provoking. Moltke was a man who took his responsibilities very seriously but who rather suffered from the feeling that he was not quite up to the job – he was lacking in strategical genius. If he now pleaded for war, this must be because of his overwhelming concern about the growing superiority of our foes.

I countered that I was not prepared to cause a preventive war, and I reminded him of Bismarck's words, that one could not see what cards were held by Providence. I was not, on the other hand, blind to the gravity of our position. And I have never rejected the idea of preventive war on principle and *a limine*. A preventive war would become the unavoidable duty of farsighted politicians in certain circumstances as a defensive war – and that is how Moltke saw it now. If war seems unavoidable, one should not allow the enemy to dictate the moment, but to decide that oneself. Even the most fanatical friend of peace will accept this rule, unless he is a completely obsessed doctrinaire. Even Bismarck's wars against Austria and France were basically preventive wars. But, quite apart from the fact that the suitable moment had perhaps passed already (at the formation of the Triple Entente, and in 1908–9, when Russia was notoriously still unprepared for war), I still had the hope that our relationship with England would improve to the extent that a general war would be virtually excluded, or at least rendered less dangerous. For once they could no longer reckon with England's active support, the Russians and the French would hardly be tempted, without this backing, to provoke a military conflict with us. Germany would automatically become ever stronger and more difficult to defeat if the peaceful development of her economic position continued. Apart from defending ourselves from our enemies we had no 'war aims', such as conquests, etc., which would justify the heavy loss of life. Finally, I was not free from concern for internal reasons with regard to a war: because of the character of the Supreme War Lord. And the Kaiser, who wanted to preserve peace, would always try to avoid war and only agree to fight if our enemies forced war upon us.

After my rejection, Moltke did not insist further with his suggestion. The idea of a war was, as already mentioned, not liked by him.

When war did break out, unexpectedly and *not* desired by us, Moltke was . . . very nervous and obviously suffering from strong depression.

In July 1914, too, I hoped that a general war would be avoided. But I cannot deny that the memory of Moltke's opinion as expressed in this conversation gave me some confidence in a victory, should such a war prove unavoidable.

E. Zechlin, 'Motive und Taktik der Reichsleitung 1914', *Der Monat*, **209**, February 1966.

8 Bethmann Hollweg's September Programme, 1914

FRITZ FISCHER

Of the many formulations of Germany's war aims in the First World War which were published by Professor Fischer in 1961, Chancellor Bethmann's programme of 9 September 1914 is generally recognized as the most important.

Expecting as he did that peace negotiations would be opening shortly, Bethmann Hollweg described his programme of 9 September as 'provisional notes on the direction of our policy on the conclusion of peace'. The 'general aim of the war' was, for him, 'security for the German Reich in west and east for all imaginable time. For this purpose France must be so weakened as to make her revival as a great power impossible for all time. Russia must be thrust back as far as possible from Germany's eastern frontier and her domination over the non-Russian vassal peoples broken.'

The objectives in the east epitomized in the lapidary last sentence of this introduction were not yet set out in detail in the programme itself, since peace with Russia was not yet regarded as imminent, but this does not mean that they had not yet assumed concrete form. The detailed enumeration of 'individual war aims' was confined to the continental west, where alone the conclusion of peace seemed within grasp. They ran as follows:

1. *France.* The military to decide whether we should demand cession of Belfort and western slopes of the Vosges, razing fortresses and cession of coastal strip from Dunkirk to Boulogne.

   The ore-field of Briey, which is necessary for the supply of ore for our industry, to be ceded in any case.

   Further, a war indemnity, to be paid in instalments; it must be high enough to prevent France from spending any considerable sums on armaments in the next fifteen–twenty years.

   Furthermore a commercial treaty which makes France economically dependent on Germany, secures the French market for our exports and makes it possible to exclude British commerce from France. This treaty must secure for us financial and industrial freedom of movement in France in such fashion that German enterprises can no longer receive different treatment from French.

2. *Belgium*. Liége and Verviers to be attached to Prussia, a frontier strip of the province of Luxemburg to Luxemburg.

Question whether Antwerp, with a corridor to Liége, should also be annexed remains open.

At any rate Belgium, even if allowed to continue to exist as a State, must be reduced to a vassal State, must allow us to occupy any militarily important ports, must place her coast at our disposal in military respects, must become economically a German province. Given such a solution, which offers the advantages of annexation without its inescapable domestic political disadvantages, French Flanders with Dunkirk, Calais and Boulogne, where most of the population is Flemish, can without danger be attached to this un-altered Belgium. The competent quarters will have to judge the military value of this position against England.

3. *Luxemburg*. Will become a German federal State and will receive a strip of the present Belgian province of Luxemburg and perhaps the corner of Longwy.

4. We must create a *central European economic association* through common customs treaties, to include France, Belgium, Holland, Denmark, Austria-Hungary, Poland (*sic*), and perhaps Italy, Sweden and Norway. This association will not have any common constitutional supreme authority and all its members will be formally equal, but in practice will be under German leadership and must stabilize Germany's economic dominance over *Mitteleuropa*.

5. *The question of colonial acquisitions*, where the first aim is the creation of a continuous Central African colonial empire, will be considered later, as will that of the aims to be realized *vis-à-vis* Russia.

6. A short provisional formula suitable for a possible preliminary peace to be found for a basis for the economic agreements to be concluded with France and Belgium.

7. *Holland*. It will have to be considered by what means and methods Holland can be brought into closer relationship with the German Empire.

In view of the Dutch character, this closer relationship must leave them free of any feeling of compulsion, must alter nothing in the Dutch way of life, and must also subject them to no new military obligations. Holland, then, must be left independent in externals, but be made internally dependent on us. Possibly one might consider an offensive and defensive alliance, to cover the colonies; in any case a close customs association, perhaps cession of Antwerp to Holland in return for the right to keep a German garrison in the fortress of Antwerp and at the mouth of the Scheldt.

Fritz Fischer, *Germany's Aims in the First World War*. Chatto & Windus, 1967, pp. 103–6.

9 Brest-Litovsk and After, 1918

FRITZ FISCHER

In this passage, Professor Fischer outlines German war aims at their fullest extent.

A survey of Germany's aims at the beginning and in the middle of 1918, when German self-confidence was at its peak in the expectation of early victory, discloses a picture of an imperium of grandiose dimensions. In the west: Belgium, Luxemburg, Longwy-Briey linked with Germany on such terms as to make possible the adherence of France and Holland and to isolate Britain and force her to recognize Germany's position; in the east: Courland, Livonia, Estonia and Lithuania, from Reval to Riga and Vilno, the Polish Frontier Strip and Rump Poland all closely fettered to Germany; in the south-east: Austria-Hungary clamped into Germany as a cornerstone, then Rumania and Bulgaria, and beyond them the Ottoman Empire as an object of Germany's Asiatic policy. Command of the eastern Mediterranean was to compel the adherence of Greece and secure the route through Suez, while the domination of the Black Sea guaranteed the economic mastery of the Ukraine, the Crimea and Georgia, and the command of the Baltic compelled Sweden and Finland, with their riches, to take the German side. On top of all this was the position of at least economic hegemony in Rump Russia.

The counterpart overseas of this European extended basis – *Mitteleuropa* surrounded by a ring of vassal States – was to be the central

Russia, and have given her a rank far above that of any European power of the old days.

F. Fischer, *Germany's Aims in the First World War.* Chatto & Windus, 1967, pp. 607 f.

10 The Secret Agreements of the Allies, 1914–18

The point has often been made that the full significance of Fischer's work on Germany's war aims will not emerge until similar studies have been undertaken on the war aims of Germany's opponents in the war. Some of the secret agreements entered into by the Entente Powers before 1917 were published by Trotsky when the Bolsheviks came to power in Russia. The texts were printed in the Manchester Guardian *in December 1917 and January and February 1918.*

1. The left bank of the Rhine
Note of the Russian Minister for Foreign Affairs of 14 February, 1917, No. 26, addressed to the French Ambassador at Petrograd:—

In your Note of today's date your Excellency was good enough to inform the Imperial Government that the Government of the Republic was contemplating the inclusion in the terms of peace to be offered to Germany the following demands and guarantees of a territorial nature:

1. Alsace-Lorraine to be restored to France.
2. The frontiers are to be extended at least up to the limits of the former principality of Lorraine, and are to be drawn up at the discretion of the French Government so as to provide for the strategical needs and for the inclusion in French territory of the entire iron district of Lorraine and of the entire coal district of the Saar valley.
3. The rest of the territories situated on the left bank of the Rhine which now form part of the German Empire are to be entirely separated from Germany and freed from all political and economic dependence upon her.

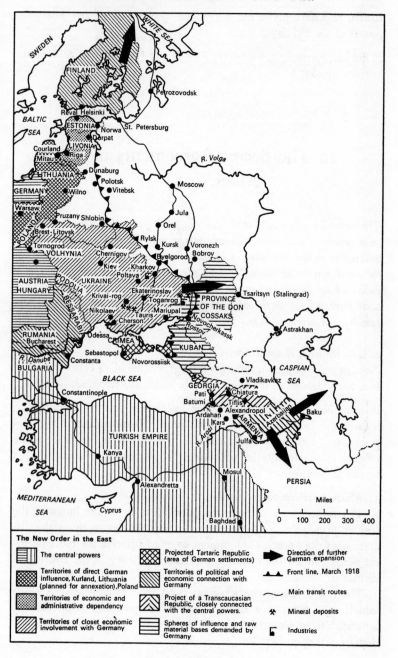

The New Order in the East

The central powers

Territories of direct German influence, Kurland, Lithuania (planned for annexation),Poland

Territories of economic and administrative dependency

Territories of closet economic involvement with Germany

Projected Tartaric Republic (area of German settlements)

Territories of political and economic connection with Germany

Project of a Transcaucasian Republic, closely connected with the central powers.

Spheres of influence and raw material bases demanded by Germany

Direction of further German expansion

Front line, March 1918

Main transit routes

Mineral deposits

Industries

77

African colonial empire safeguarded by naval bases and linked with the Near East through the Sudan and Suez. With this economic and political power in Africa, reinforced by the command of the strategic and technical key-points on the route to South America to expand and consolidate the strong economic interests already established there before the war, Germany was to make herself a colonial and economic power of world status. Yet concentration on the African empire implied no withdrawal from the eastern hemisphere. Germany was maintaining her interests in Samoa and New Guinea and trying to initiate in China a more elastic policy, confined purely to the safeguarding of her economic interests. Above all, she hoped that by ceding Kiaochow to Japan she would be able to renew her old connections with that country against both Russia and the Anglo-Saxon powers.

Germany's political and economic imperium would have represented a concentration of force far surpassing Bismarck's empire in resources and human material. The old industrial areas of the Ruhr and Luxemburg, the Saar, German Lorraine, Saxony and Upper Silesia were to be reinforced by French Lorraine, Belgium, Poland and Bohemia. For her supply of ore, besides her own production and the assured imports from Sweden, she could have drawn on the ores of Austria, Poland, Longwy-Briey, the Ukraine, the Caucasus, Turkey and Katanga. To the oil of Galicia was added that of Rumania, the Caucasus and Mesopotamia, to her own agricultural production that of the Balkans and the north-east, to her previous imports from her old colonies in Africa, the abundant produce of central Africa; markets previously contested would be replaced by near-monopoly in Georgia, Turkey, Russia, the Ukraine, the Balkans, the north-east, the north and the west. The weight of the German Reich in matters of commercial policy would unquestionably have put Germany in an impregnable position of world-economic power. The economic agreements were, moreover, to be safeguarded by military treaties.

Military conventions with Finland, the Baltic States, Lithuania, Poland, the Ukraine, Georgia, Turkey, Bulgaria, Rumania and Austria-Hungary, and in a negative sense also with Belgium, had been planned, and most of them at least initialled. Through these economic, political and military links Germany would have created a European bloc which would have put her on a level with the three world powers of America, Britain and – if she could still be counted –

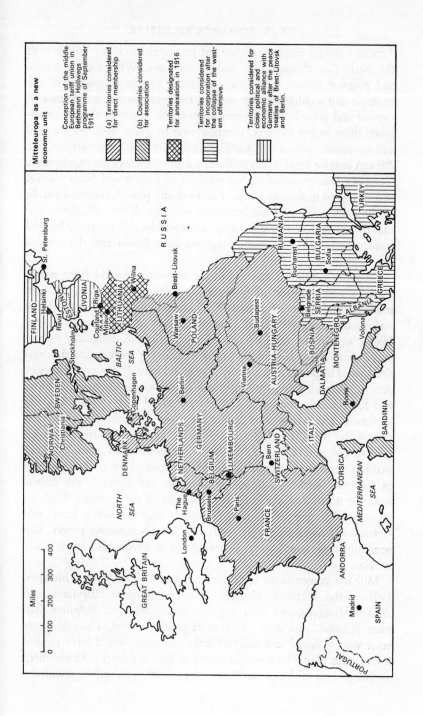

Mitteleuropa as a new
economic unit

Conception of the middle
European tariff union in
Bethmann Hollwegs
programme of September
1914

(a) Territories considered
for direct membership

(b) Countries considered
for association

Territories designated
for annexation in 1916

Territories considered
for incorporation after
the collapse of the west-
ern offensive.

Territories considered for
close political and
economic alliance with
Germany after the peace
treaties of Brest-Litovsk
and Berlin.

Russia, and have given her a rank far above that of any European power of the old days.

F. Fischer, *Germany's Aims in the First World War*. Chatto & Windus, 1967, pp. 607 f.

10 The Secret Agreements of the Allies, 1914–18

The point has often been made that the full significance of Fischer's work on Germany's war aims will not emerge until similar studies have been undertaken on the war aims of Germany's opponents in the war. Some of the secret agreements entered into by the Entente Powers before 1917 were published by Trotsky when the Bolsheviks came to power in Russia. The texts were printed in the Manchester Guardian in December 1917 and January and February 1918.

1. *The left bank of the Rhine*

Note of the Russian Minister for Foreign Affairs of 14 February, 1917, No. 26, addressed to the French Ambassador at Petrograd:—

In your Note of today's date your Excellency was good enough to inform the Imperial Government that the Government of the Republic was contemplating the inclusion in the terms of peace to be offered to Germany the following demands and guarantees of a territorial nature:

1. Alsace-Lorraine to be restored to France.
2. The frontiers are to be extended at least up to the limits of the former principality of Lorraine, and are to be drawn up at the discretion of the French Government so as to provide for the strategical needs and for the inclusion in French territory of the entire iron district of Lorraine and of the entire coal district of the Saar valley.
3. The rest of the territories situated on the left bank of the Rhine which now form part of the German Empire are to be entirely separated from Germany and freed from all political and economic dependence upon her.

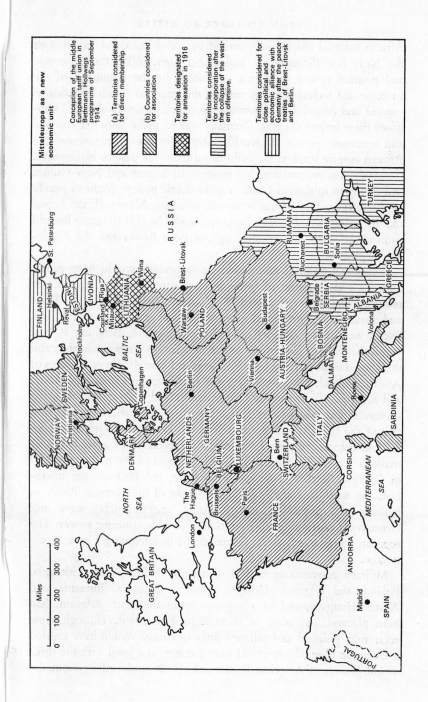

Mitteleuropa as a new economic unit

Conception of the middle European tariff union in Bethmann Hollwegs programme of September 1914

(a) Territories considered for direct membership

(b) Countries considered for association

Territories designated for annexation in 1916

Territories considered for incorporation after the collapse of the western offensive

Territories considered for close political and economic alliance with Germany at the peace treaties of Brest-Litovsk and Berlin.

African colonial empire safeguarded by naval bases and linked with the Near East through the Sudan and Suez. With this economic and political power in Africa, reinforced by the command of the strategic and technical key-points on the route to South America to expand and consolidate the strong economic interests already established there before the war, Germany was to make herself a colonial and economic power of world status. Yet concentration on the African empire implied no withdrawal from the eastern hemisphere. Germany was maintaining her interests in Samoa and New Guinea and trying to initiate in China a more elastic policy, confined purely to the safeguarding of her economic interests. Above all, she hoped that by ceding Kiaochow to Japan she would be able to renew her old connections with that country against both Russia and the Anglo-Saxon powers.

Germany's political and economic imperium would have represented a concentration of force far surpassing Bismarck's empire in resources and human material. The old industrial areas of the Ruhr and Luxemburg, the Saar, German Lorraine, Saxony and Upper Silesia were to be reinforced by French Lorraine, Belgium, Poland and Bohemia. For her supply of ore, besides her own production and the assured imports from Sweden, she could have drawn on the ores of Austria, Poland, Longwy-Briey, the Ukraine, the Caucasus, Turkey and Katanga. To the oil of Galicia was added that of Rumania, the Caucasus and Mesopotamia, to her own agricultural production of the Balkans and the north-east, to her previous imports from her old colonies in Africa, the abundant produce of central Africa; markets previously contested would be replaced by near-monopoly in Georgia, Turkey, Russia, the Ukraine, the Balkans, the north-east, the north and the west. The weight of the German Reich in matters of commercial policy would unquestionably have put Germany in an impregnable position of world-economic power. The economic agreements were, moreover, to be safeguarded by military treaties.

Military conventions with Finland, the Baltic States, Lithuania, Poland, the Ukraine, Georgia, Turkey, Bulgaria, Rumania and Austria-Hungary, and in a negative sense also with Belgium, had been planned, and most of them at least initialled. Through these economic, political and military links Germany would have created a European bloc which would have put her on a level with the three world powers of America, Britain and – if she could still be counted –

The New Order in the East

- The central powers
- Territories of direct German influence, Kurland, Lithuania (planned for annexation), Poland
- Territories of economic and administrative dependency
- Territories of closet economic involvement with Germany
- Projected Tartaric Republic (area of German settlements)
- Territories of political and economic connection with Germany
- Project of a Transcaucasian Republic, closely connected with the central powers.
- Spheres of influence and raw material bases demanded by Germany
- Direction of further German expansion
- Front line, March 1918
- Main transit routes
- Mineral deposits
- Industries

4. The territories on the left bank of the Rhine outside French territory are to be constituted an autonomous and neutral State, and are to be occupied by French troops until such time as the enemy States have completely satisfied all the conditions and guarantees indicated in the treaty of peace.

Your Excellency stated that the Government of the Republic would be happy to be able to rely upon the support of the Imperial Government for the carrying out of its plans. By order of his Imperial Majesty, my most august master, I have the honour, in the name of the Russian Government, to inform your Excellency by the present Note that the Government of the Republic may rely upon the support of the Imperial Government for the carrying out of its plans as set out above.

(*Manchester Guardian*, 12 December 1917)

2. Poland and Russia's western frontiers

From a confidential telegram from M. Sazonoff (Russian Foreign Minister) to the Russian Ambassador in Paris, 9 March 1916, No. 948. At the forthcoming conference you may be guided by the following general principles: All suggestions for the future delimitation of central Europe are at present premature, but in general one must bear in mind that we are prepared to allow France and England complete freedom in drawing up the western frontiers of Germany, in the expectation that the allies on their part would allow us equal freedom in drawing up our frontiers with Germany and Austria. It is particularly necessary to insist on the exclusion of the Polish question from the subject of international discussion and on the elimination of all attempts to place the future of Poland under the guarantee and the control of the powers.

(*Manchester Guardian*, 12 December 1917)

Telegram from the Russian Ambassador in Paris, 11 March 1917, No. 168

The Government of the French Republic, anxious to confirm the importance of the treaties concluded with the Russian Government in 1916 for the settlement on the termination of the war of the question of Constantinople and the Straits in accordance with Russia's aspirations, anxious, on the other hand, to secure for its ally in military and industrial respects all the guarantees desirable for the safety and the economic development of the Empire, recognises Russia's complete liberty in establishing her western frontiers.

(Signed) Isvolsky
(*Manchester Guardian*, 12 December 1917)

3. Constantinople and the Straits

From an undated Memorandum forming one of a series of Russian diplomatic documents published by the *Izvestiya* on 23 November 1917.

On 4 March 1915, a memorandum was handed by the Minister for Foreign Affairs to the French and British Ambassadors, in which was set forth the desire for the annexation, as a result of the present war, of the following territories: the town of Constantinople, the western shores of the Bosphorus, of the Sea of Marmora, and of the Dardanelles, Southern Thrace up to the line of Enos-Midia, the shores of Asia Minor between the Bosphorus, the River Sakaria, and some point on the Gulf of Izmid, which was reserved for closer definition, the Islands of the Sea of Marmora, and the Islands of Imbros and Tenedos. The special rights of France and England within the limits of these territories were not to be infringed.

The British as well as the French Government declared their consent to the fulfilment of our wishes, on the conditions of a successful conclusion of the war, and of the fulfilment of a series of French and English claims, both within the limits of the Ottoman Empire and elsewhere.

These claims, as far as they concern Turkey, may be summarized as follows: the recognition of Constantinople as a free port for the transit of merchandise not coming from Russia nor going into Russia, and the free transit of merchant ships through the Straits.

The recognition of certain rights of England and France in Asiatic Turkey, which rights are reserved for more precise definition by means of a special agreement between France, England and Russia.

The placing of the sacred Mussulman places and Arabia under an independent Mussulman rule.

The inclusion within the English sphere of influence of the neutral zone of Persia (as established by the agreement between England and Russia in 1907).

IV
The Improvised Revolution of 1918

By 1918, especially after the failure of Ludendorff's Spring Offensive, Germany began to crack under the strain of four years of total war. Public opinion, which was in any case demanding an increasing say in the running of the country's affairs, turned more and more against the Kaiser, who was regarded as an obstacle to peace especially after President Wilson made it clear that he would negotiate only with a representative government. There was, however, little desire for a socialist revolution. Trade union leaders had warned their members as early as April 1917, before the Bolshevik take-over in Russia, that Germany was not Russia, and that the 'revolutionary games of the Independents and Spartacists [the later Communists] endangered the German labour movement'. In the army, as in the labour movement, there were two streams: on the one hand men like Ludendorff and Colonel Max Bauer who were already toying with the ideas of Gottfried Feder, the young Munich engineer who helped to write the first Nazi Party programme, and on the other hand men like General Groener, who had genuinely good relations with the Social Democrats and were outraged by the 'unheard-of manner' in which many industrialists were engaging in 'mad profit-making'. The alliance of 1918 between the moderate army leaders and the moderate Social-ist leaders against the – real or imagined – threat of Bolshevism and chaos ensured a large degree of continuity with the past. The Kaiser and the other monarchs abdicated, but the States they had ruled, together with the bureaucracies of those States, survived. The nucleus of the old Prussian army survived, and soon hardly bothered to conceal its contempt for the party politicians who held office. On the indus-trial front, a parallel alliance between employers and trade unions gave the workers certain rights for which they had been fighting for decades, but no parts of German industry – not even the coal mines – came under public ownership. Women were given the vote, and the parties changed their names to accord with the 'democratic' spirit of the times, but their attitudes remained conditioned by their experiences under the old régime. There was, then, a break in continuity in 1918, but that break was superficial, and it was only a question of time before the old forces began to reassert themselves. As the left-wing Socialist, Gustav Landauer, wrote to a colleague in the capital on 12 November 1918, three days after the Kaiser's abdication and the proclamation of the Republic: 'I am still very dissatisfied with Berlin. You with your damned continuity.'

1 The Majority Socialists try to Save the Monarchy, 1918

COLONEL HANS VON HAEFTEN

On 6 November 1918, General Groener met the leaders of the Social Democrats and the trade unions, who all urged him – in vain – to advise the Kaiser to abdicate so as to save the monarchy.

The invited gentlemen appeared at the appointed time, except for Ebert and Groener. The start of the discussion was therefore delayed until their arrival half an hour later. During this time I could hear a telephone conversation which Scheidemann was having with Noske, who was in Kiel. Here Noske described the situation in Kiel as almost hopeless. General chaos was near, and power was passing more and more into the hands of the revolutionary sailors. The excitement of the past few days had completely exhausted and sickened him, so that he was forced to take to his bed.

When all the gentleman had arrived, Ebert began by briefly describing the situation. This was not the time to look for those who were responsible for the general collapse. But the people were widely convinced that the Kaiser was the guilty one, and whether or not this was justified was immaterial at the present time. The main thing was that the people wanted to see the man they held responsible for the disaster removed from his post. Consequently the abdication of the Kaiser was absolutely necessary if one wanted to prevent the masses from going over to the revolutionary camp, and thus prevent revolution itself. He proposed that the Kaiser should voluntarily declare his abdication today, or at the latest tomorrow, and entrust one of his sons – perhaps Prince Eitel Friedrich or Prince Oskar – with the regency. The Crown Prince was at the present moment 'impossible' because he was hated by the masses. General Groener answered curtly and sharply that there could be no thought of the Kaiser's abdication. At the present time, when the army was locked in the last and difficult combat with the enemy, it was impossible to deprive it of its Supreme War Lord and thus of its authoritative support. So long as we were still fighting the external enemy the interests of the army must come before all else. He therefore refused most decisively to take any step whatever in the abdication question, let alone to suggest anything of the sort to the Kaiser.

The deputies David and Südekum then tried again to explain to General Groener the necessity and urgency of the abdication. Both declared that they were by no means opponents of monarchy in itself, and that this step would by no means imply the removal of the monarchy. Large sections of German Social Democracy would be prepared to accept a monarchic state with a parliamentary system.

During the almost scholarly arguments of the deputy David, State Secretary Scheidemann was called to the telephone. He returned after a few minutes, as white as a sheet and shaking all over, and interrupted David with the words: 'The abdication question is now no longer of any importance. The revolution is on the march. I have just been told that numerous Kiel sailors have arrested the governors in Hamburg and Hanover and taken over the government themselves. That means: revolution!'

In the face of Scheidemann's excitement, Ebert remained unshakeably cool. He declared that nothing had yet been settled. Concerning the monarchy, he and Scheidemann were in fact convinced republicans, but the question: monarchy or republic, was at the present of only theoretical interest. In practice they too would agree to a monarchy with a parliamentary system. He therefore pressed General Groener urgently to seize the last opportunity to save the monarchy and to arrange for the speedy establishment of the regency of one of the Imperial Princes. Deputy Südekum supported Ebert's view with moving words, and with tears in his eyes and emotion in his voice he begged General Groener to accept Ebert's proposals. Otherwise we would be faced by a terrible catastrophe 'whose consequences none of us could foresee'. Legien too spoke in this sense.

Here General Groener answered briefly and very definitely, almost rudely, that the proposal was out of the question for him. He had been authorized to tell the gentlemen that all the Imperial Princes had declared their solidarity with their father, and that none of the Princes was ready to accept the regency should his father be forced to abdicate against his will. On hearing this Ebert rose immediately and said: 'In these circumstances there is no point in further discussion, now things will have to take their course.' And, turning to General Groener, he concluded: 'We thank you, Excellency, for the frank conversation and we shall always gladly recall our cooperation with you during the war. From now on our paths will diverge. Who knows if we shall ever meet again.'

... When the gentlemen had all left the room I said to General Groener: 'That means revolution – these leaders no longer have the masses under control. If you don't do as they say the generals will be without troops.'

Printed in Gerhard A. Ritter and Susanne Miller, *Die deutsche Revolution 1918-19*. Frankfurt, 1968, pp. 50 ff.

2 The Kaiser Decides against Civil War, 1918

COUNT KUNO VON WESTARP

At the Supreme Headquarters in Spa, Belgium, the Kaiser wanted to march back into Germany at the head of the army to put down the revolution. General Groener had to inform him on 9 November 1918 that the troops would no longer obey their commanders in such an action. They would, however, maintain discipline under their leaders if the Kaiser abdicated. The Prussian army jettisoned the Kaiser in order to preserve itself.

In face of the ever-growing revolutionary movement His Majesty was firmly determined not to give way, recognizing that his abdication would lead to the disintegration of the nation and the army. On the morning of 8 November he expressed his intention of restoring order at home at the head of the army. General Groener was commanded to prepare the operation.

On the evening of 8 November this matter was discussed by Field-Marshal von Hindenburg, Colonel-General von Plessen and Lieutenant-General Groener. The situation was then as follows:

News had arrived that the workers' and soldiers' councils had seized power in the big cities, on the coast, in the west and the south. The Rhine front, and the big ammunition dumps which had been positioned on and behind this line because of the approaching armistice, as well as the important railway junctions of the homeland, were in the hands of the revolutionaries. The food and munition supplies of the field were sufficient only for a few more days, whereas supplies from the interior had already been stopped several times, for example, in Cologne and Munich. The occupation forces in the homeland had gone over to the revolution almost without exception, and those troops which had been sent there and had been described by their commanders as absolutely reliable had immediately succumbed to the evil influences of the homeland. ...

In view of these circumstances General Groener described the plan of marching against the homeland as hopeless. The decisive factor was that not all troops were ready and suitable for fighting the revolution at home. The speedy discovery, consolidation and deployment of reliable troops would have been extremely difficult in view of their dispersal in the wide areas between the Channel and Switzerland, even where – which was mostly the case – they were not locked in conflict with the enemy. One could not rely on the possibility that the activities in the homeland would be limited to minor skirmishes. Rather one would have to be prepared for serious battles on the strong Rhine front, when crossing Germany, and in Berlin, that is, over an area of some 600 kilometres. To oppose the rebels, who included trained and well-armed troops and who had occupied various strongholds, stronger formations would have been necessary than would have been quickly assembled even in the best of circumstances, as well as far more ammunition and food than was available. On top of the unavoidable civil war the continuation of the bloody fight with the Entente would be necessary, for the Entente would undoubtedly press on from the west.

Field-Marshal von Hindenburg supported with a heavy heart this judgement of General Groener's, which was based on the most careful analysis of the situation. In the given circumstances there would be no expectation of success; on the contrary every responsible adviser would see that complete collapse would be the undoubted result of the entire plan.

Colonel-General von Plessen, on the other hand, expressed the view that it was intolerable for the Kaiser and the army to give way to a handful of revolutionaries. The Fatherland would not understand why the army that for four years had earned the admiration of the whole world was now incapable of dealing with a band of vicious sailors.

The Field-Marshal and General Groener, while fully respecting the sentiments of the Colonel-General, felt obliged to stick to their opinion. . . .

On 9 November, at 10 a.m., the Field-Marshal and General Groener [and five others] reported to His Majesty on the military position. . . .

At the start of the audience the Field-Marshal begged His Majesty to be relieved of his post, for the thought of having to advise his War Lord against a decision which he greeted with joy in his heart but whose implementation, after careful consideration, he must describe as impossible, was unbearable. His Majesty reserved his position. General Groener then described the above situation and declared the idea of an action by the field army against the homeland . . . to be impracticable. The Field-Marshal supported these views.

During this report and also afterwards General Count Schulenburg and Colonel-General von Plessen expressed the contrary opinion. . . .

His Majesty at first inclined towards the Plessen-Schulenburg view, but finally decided that the plan to conquer the homeland through operation of the field army must be abandoned. The Kaiser wanted to spare the Fatherland a civil war, and the army – after all its heroically-borne suffering and losses – further campaigns. His Majesty now expressed the intention of returning peacefully to the homeland at the head of the army as soon as the armistice was signed. This idea too was declared by General Groener to be impracticable, because the whole revolution had turned directly against the person of the Kaiser. He declared 'The army will march back in peace and order to the homeland under its leaders and commanding generals, but not under the command of Your Majesty; for it no longer stands behind Your Majesty!'

The question of His Majesty's abdication was not touched upon during the report on the military situation. Not until the end of this report did the first demand for his abdication arrive from the Reich Chancellery in Berlin. The demands were then repeated with ever-greater urgency, so that the military report had to be stopped. His Majesty moved with those present into the park. . . .

Kuno Graf von Westarp, *Das Ende der Monarchie am 9. November 1918*. Berlin, 1952, pp. 42–8.

3 Groener's Alliance with Ebert, 1918

WILHELM GROENER

The Social Democrat Scheidemann proclaimed the Republic in Berlin on 9 November 1918. Late on 10 November, General Groener established a secret telephone link with Ebert, the Socialist leader, and proposed an alliance between the officer corps and the majority socialists against Bolshevism.

The duty of the army command was now to lead the rest of the army speedily and in an orderly fashion, and above all sound in mind and body, back into the homeland. It was also to enable the officer corps, as the bearer of the military tradition, to find its feet in the new situation. The moral and spiritual power which had collected in the Prussian-German officer corps over the centuries had to be preserved, in its essence, for the army of the future. The collapse of the Kaiserdom deprived the officers of the basis of their existence, of their loyalties and sense of direction. They had to be given an aim for which they could fight and which would restore their self-confidence. A sense of duty had to be awakened in them not only towards a particular political structure but towards Germany as a whole. That Hindenburg stayed at his post and took over supreme command of the entire army, indeed that this command was bestowed upon him by the Kaiser, facilitated the transition.

The officer corps could, however, only cooperate with a government which took up the fight against radicalism and Bolshevism. Ebert accepted this, but he was in grave danger of losing control and close to being overrun by the Independents and the Liebknecht group. What could be more logical than to offer Ebert – whom I knew to be an upright and reliable character and the most politically farsighted of his army of comrades – the support of the army and the officer corps?

...In the evening [10 November 1918] I telephoned the Reich Chancellery and told Ebert that the army put itself at the disposal of the government, that in return for this the Field-Marshal and the officer corps expected the support of the government in the mainten-ance of order and discipline in the army. The officer corps expected the government to fight against Bolshevism and was ready for the struggle. Ebert accepted my offer of an alliance. From then on we discussed the measures which were necessary every evening on a secret telephone line between the Reich Chancellery and the high command. The alliance proved successful.

We [the high command] hoped through our action to gain a share of the power in the new State for the army and the officer corps. If we succeeded, then we would have rescued into the new Germany the best and strongest element of old Prussia, despite the revolution.

At first, of course, we had to make concessions, for developments in the army and in the homeland had taken such a turn as to make the vigorous issuing of commands by the high command impossible for the time being. The task was to contain and render harmless the revolutionary movement.

Wilhelm Groener, *Lebenserinnerungen. Jugend, Generalstab, Weltkrieg.* Göttingen, 1957, pp. 467 ff.

4 The Terms of the Alliance, 1918

PAUL VON HINDENBURG

In a letter to Ebert of 8 December 1918, Hindenburg elaborated the army's demands. The letter was almost certainly written by Groener.

If I address myself to you as follows, I am doing so because I have been told that you too as a loyal German love your Fatherland more than anything else.... In this sense I have allied myself with you to save the nation from threatening disaster ...

If the army is to remain a usable instrument of power in the hands of the government, the authority of the officer has to be restored immediately by every means, and politics have to be eliminated from the army. This requires a decree of the government which stipulates clearly:

1. The right to issue military commands rests solely with the commanding authorities.
2. The authority of the officers and the regulations connected with it must be completely restored. In particular I should like to point out the absolute necessity of the duty to salute, which is of decisive importance for the maintenance of discipline. . . .
3. The soldiers' councils must disappear from the units; only *Vertrauensräte* are permissible, which should inform the commanding officers of the mood of the other ranks and transmit their wishes and complaints. A participation of the *Vertrauensräte* in the issuing of military orders is out of the question.

These are the military demands. But I feel obliged to inform you about the mood which is shown in numerous communications from the field army and all other groups of the population. This amounts above all to the demand that the National Assembly must be summoned *at once*. . . .

I am convinced that only the following measures can help us to overcome the present difficulties:

1. Summoning of the National Assembly in the course of December.
2. Until then, or until the decision of the National Assembly can be carried out, conduct of the administration solely by the government and the legitimate administrative organs.
3. So as to fulfil the justified wishes of the working class . . . qualified people of working class origin should be attached to the administrative authorities in an advisory capacity. These should not form an independent 'council' but should work together with the authorities. The need of 'workers' councils' would thus be eliminated.
4. The security service must be solely in the hands of the legal police organs and of the armed forces.
5. Safeguarding of the orders of the government by a reliable police force and, after the restoration of discipline, by the army.

In your hands lies the fate of the German nation. It will depend on your decision whether the German nation will rise once more. I am prepared, and with me the whole army, to support you without any reservation.

F. L. Carsten, *The Reichswehr and Politics*, Oxford University Press, 1966, pp. 13–14.

5 The Survival of the Bureaucracy, 1918

FRIEDRICH EBERT

Once in power, the Majority Socialists discovered that they were to a large degree dependent on the expert advice of the old Imperial bureaucracy. Ebert described the situation in a speech to the Prime Ministers of the German States on 25 November 1918.

I should like to make some comments on the nature of the Reich Government, because it seems that not everyone is very clear on this score. When we took the Government we worked on the assumption that the entire political leadership of the Reich had been placed in the hands of the Council of People's Commissars. This Council consists entirely of representatives of the Socialist parties. All political decisions of the Reich lie in the hands of this body. But, gentlemen, you must remember one thing: the Reich machine is rather more complicated than that of even the biggest of our federal States. We had to make sure, once we had taken over political power, that the Reich machine did not break down. (Quite right!) We had to make sure that the machine continued to operate so as to be able to maintain our food supplies and the economy. (Renewed agreement!) And that was not an easy task. We worked with all our strength day and night so as to prevent collapse and downfall within a few days. (Quite right!) The six of us could not do that alone; we needed the experienced cooperation of experts. Had we removed the experienced heads of the Reich Offices, had we replaced them with people who did not possess the necessary knowledge and experience, then we should have faced failure within a few days. (Quite right!) We therefore urgently appealed to all Reich officials to continue to exercise their duty until further notice. Only in that way was it possible to avoid collapse and surmount the difficulties. (Renewed agreement!)

Ritter and Miller, *Die deutsche Revolution*, pp. 320 f.

6 The Alliance between Employers and Trade Unions, 1918

HANS VON RAUMER

Parallel to the alliance between Groener and Ebert there took place an almost equally decisive alliance between the big industrialists and the trade union leaders. The general aim of the industrialists was similar to that of the Army Command: to prevent outright revolution by making timely concessions to the moderates. Here one of the industrialists describes the negotiations of October–December 1918.

The suggestion which I made in July 1918 to some of the leaders of the finished-product industry, to establish organic links with the trade unions before we were swept away by the flood of events, was accepted, and I undertook the preparatory negotiations with everyone's approval. Because of sickness and other reasons, a delay occurred until 2 October. On that day I met the chairman of the Free Trade Unions, Carl Legien, his deputy, Gustav Bauer, and August (*sic*) Schlicke from the Metalworker's Union, in the house of State Secretary August Müller. A harmonious cooperation was only possible – this I had agreed with the industrialists – on the basis of complete parity. Complete parity had been the aim of trade union policy and so it was not surprising that my offer aroused a joyful readiness to negotiate. Typical of the atmosphere of that time were the words uttered by Legien on our homeward journey: 'And even if nothing more results from the whole business than that we should meet informally around a table every four weeks, a great deal will have been achieved.'

The negotiations with the leading employers which we had arranged on 2 October took place at my house on 22 October 1918. I only had a small smoking room at my disposal, so that the eleven participants had to sit squashed together. But perhaps this familiar proximity created a better atmosphere than would have been the case if we had sat formally around a table in a larger hall. . . . Since complete parity in all common organizations formed the basis of the negotiations, the demands of the trade unions were accepted virtually without discussion. Agreement was reached on the following points: recognition of the trade unions as the official representatives of the workers, unlimited right of association, the formation of labour exchanges and arbitration boards on a parity basis, the signing of wage agreements in the individual branches of industry and finally the dropping by the employers of the so-called 'yellow unions'. Agreement was further reached that all the problems resulting from the end of the war would be settled jointly on a parity basis.

A few days later, on my invitation, Hugo Stinnes joined our circle and together with Legien he took the lead. The joint leadership of these two men was most successful. An unconditional relationship of trust immediately arose between these extraordinary men, both of whom thought in uncomplicated, realistic terms. Carl Legien had taken over the chairmanship of the General Committee of the Free Trade Unions in 1890, after the lapsing of the Anti-Socialist law, and his leadership of the whole movement thereafter was never questioned. His personality had much in common with Friedrich Ebert's. He was a man of statesmanlike greatness, with an iron, but strictly controlled, will, and of unqualified honesty. . . . His life's purpose was to improve the condition of the working class, and he pursued this aim realistically and completely undogmatically. That gave him the freedom to drop all ideas of a class struggle and to put himself fully behind the cooperation with the employers.

Political events made speed imperative. The first question to be dealt with was what would happen to the army if and when the Kaiser and Crown Prince abdicated. Hugo Stinnes, Legien, Bauer and I arranged to discuss this question with General Ludendorff, who had just returned from the front, on 30 October. We believed that a chaotic flooding back of troops could only be avoided if Field-Marshal von Hindenburg led the army back home in person. Ludendorff objected that Hindenburg had the moral duty to resign together with him, and he for his part had to submit his resignation immediately. We finally managed to persuade Ludendorff to telephone Hindenburg

on the following day, saying that in the interests of the Fatherland
he must stay at his post. The political views of the two trade union
leaders, as they emerged in this discussion, were very interesting.
They did not want the removal of the monarchy, but a parliamentary
régime with a regency council, including some trade unionists, to
take over the government until the eldest son of the Crown Prince
came of age.

The next meeting took place on 2 November. Representatives of
the other trade unions, above all Stegerwald, now also took part in the
discussions. It was agreed to demand the setting up of a separate Reich
Office for Demobilization, and to give it extensive powers. . . .
The demand was formulated and signed that night, and I was charged
with the job of getting the document to the Reich Chancellor the
next day. In the Reich Chancellery I was received by the Vice-
Chancellor von Payer, who was deputizing for the Chancellor who
was ill. To his somewhat sceptical question as to whom I represented
I could reply: 'I represent the only power which still exists in Germany
today, the united employers and employees of Germany.'

The revolutionary days of 9 and 10 November interrupted our
work. But on 11 November we met once again. The revolution had
decisively altered the balance of power between the two sides. The
trade unions made new demands, especially the introduction of the
eight-hour day for all industries. The alliance seemed in danger of
collapse at the last minute. Hugo Stinnes saved the situation by declaring: 'Today you have political power in your hands, but I will sign
nothing that I am not prepared fully to support even in altered political
circumstances.' And here Legien intervened. The voluntary, unconditional offer of the employers, which until then had met with the
complete approval of the trade unions, must not, he felt, be jeopardized
by exploiting a momentary political situation to one's own advantage.
Thus agreement was reached on the eight-hour day . . . but this
was made acceptable to the employers by the conclusion of a separate
agreement, to the effect that its introduction would be dependent
upon its international acceptance. . . . On 15 November all the trade
unions gave their approval to the agreement, which has rightly been
called the Magna Carta of the trade unions. The employers' associations
also signed on 15 November.

Thus, in the space of less than three weeks, we had achieved full
agreement and had prepared the ground for that cooperation which
established order in the following few years. Seven employers had

effected this change without any kind of mandate from the employers' associations, yet it was a change which revolutionized the previous relationship between employers and trade unions. . . .

It is no exaggeration to say that this cooperation . . . saved Germany in the early years from chaos and from Bolshevik revolution. When all authority had collapsed: monarchy, State, army and bureaucracy, the alliance of the employers with the trade unions formed a power which maintained order in the economy. What happened in all other revolutions, that the workers turned against the employers, did not happen here because the unions cooperated with the employers in the preservation of order.

Ritter and Miller, *Die deutsche Revolution*, pp. 210–14.

7 Democracy or Dictatorship, 1918

HUGO PREUSS

Would cooperation between the Social Democrats and the extreme Left in 1918 have averted the rise of Nazi dictatorship in later years? The question, which is often asked, is of hypothetical interest only, for the hostility between the two sides of the Socialist movement was a historical reality which cannot be thought away from the situation of 1918. Even if such an alliance had come about, however, it might have been short-lived, for – as Hugo Preuss, the architect of the Weimar Constitution, argued in this article of 14 November 1918 – the result might well have been Jacobin terror followed by military dictatorship.

Only a few days have passed since the fall of the old autocratic system in Germany; so far, at any rate, this change has taken place with an orderliness which is truly surprising and wonderful in a revolution of such tremendous significance; – and yet even today one hears an ever-increasing number of voices expressing something like home-sickness for the old autocracy. . . . That is psychologically understandable but politically absurd. For the rottenness of that autocracy was the cause of its bankruptcy and of the present revolution; it is also, however, the cause of the fact that the autocracy has so far not been replaced by a democracy but by an inverted autocratic system. In the old autocracy the citizen had very little to say, in the present one he has absolutely none; more than ever the people as a whole is purely the object of a government which imposes upon it decisions arrived at in a mysterious way. The only difference is that these decisions are no longer justified in terms of the grace of God, but in terms of the – just as vague – will of the people. . . . In short, this is quite simply the autocratic State turned upside down.

True, one could say to the bourgeoisie . . . that it has no right to complain about this exclusion, since its political sins of omission, its weakness and servility, carry a goodly share of the responsibility for the rottenness of the old order and consequently for the present collapse. It is also undoubtedly true that the bourgeoisie and the old political parties could never by themselves have brought about a change such as the one we are now witnessing; and it is therefore understandable that the organizers of the revolution wish to enjoy its fruits alone. But opposed to this wish stands the fact that that would make the development of political liberty, which is after all the declared aim of the revolution, an impossibility. Not only that, but the entire future of our already long-suffering German people would be delivered into destruction.

Yes, the so-called policies of the old parties and their leaders were miserable, just as miserable as the policies and the leaders of the old autocracy. . . . But the question of guilt is not now important. . . . The aims of the present holders of power might be the best and most pure imaginable; yet they cannot escape from the logic of the situation, which is that the attempt to constitute the new State while excluding its bourgeoisie must lead unavoidably, within a short space of time, to Bolshevik terror. The present solution, in which numerous bourgeois elements continue to carry out their public duties under the dictatorship of an autocracy to which they are fundamentally opposed, may work as an emergency measure; but that can last for a short while only, and will soon be considered unbearable by either one side or the other. If by that time a democratic political organization has not been established to secure equal rights for all citizens, then there will be no alternative to violence, and with it the complete ruin of our economic life. He who dreams of establishing the general dictatorship of the international proletariat by destroying all community relationships within the nation might perhaps be prepared to pursue such a course; but never he who wants to establish, in the midst of this great collapse, a democratic German republic to which those parts still outside will wish voluntarily and joyfully to adhere. This is the complete and immediate parting of the ways. The question here is 'Eastern or Western orientation', in a new and fateful sense. How the reactionaries have tried to arouse our disgust at the 'Western democracies'; and not only some Liberals but also some Social Democrats have swallowed the bait. Do we now, instead of this, want to imitate Bolshevism, the negative plate of Russian tsarism? . . . Albert Thomas has just written in *Humanité*: 'Either Wilson or Lenin, either democracy as it has developed out of the French and American revolutions or the brutal form of Russian fanaticism. That is the choice'.

If it were the inevitable fate of all revolutions that the Gironde must be overrun by the Jacobin reign of terror, then it is its fate to give away to a sabre-rattling régime which acts as the saviour of society. That things need not necessarily run that course is shown by English and American history. For the future course of events in our country, the attitude and mood of the bourgeoisie will surely be of great significance. We can escape from the dreadful alternation of red and white terror only if a strong and energetic movement within the German bourgeoisie stands firmly behind the accomplished facts, but not if it bows its head tamely under the new autocracy as it has done for so long – to the disadvantage of the German people – under the old. . . . The bourgeoisie must not, nor does it wish to, become the vanguard of reaction; it wishes to go hand in hand with the new forces, not as a lackey but as an equal partner. Not classes and groups, not parties and estates in hostile isolation, but only the whole German people, represented by a German National Assembly elected by completely democratic elections, can create the German republic. And that must be created quickly if unspeakable misfortune is not to crush completely our poor people.

Ritter and Miller, *Die deutsche Revolution*, pp. 292–4.

8 A Republic Divides Us Least, 1918

FRIEDRICH MEINECKE

This article, written by Meinecke in November 1918, shows how many liberal intellectuals accepted the Republic, if only because a monarchist restoration would now mean dictatorship.

Is democratic-parliamentary monarchy still thinkable and practicable? Our natural line of development during the war appeared to be pointing in that direction and we had actually achieved that solution through the October reforms of Prince Max's Chancellorship. I would have greeted it as a priceless stroke of good fortune if we had been able to achieve what the English have so far managed to achieve, namely to preserve the historical connection with the past, the continuity of constitutional and legal evolution, in the midst of the most radical and fundamental change. The atmosphere is too rare, too thin, too cold, in a political structure which has been purged entirely of traditional values.

But it was not to be. True, there is no doubt that the vast majority of the German people is still monarchist today. But the monarchy itself delivered the deathblow to its prospects by the undignified manner of its end, and by the complete inadequacy of the last emperor. Now that monarchy has through its own fault collapsed at the centre, it can no longer survive in the separate States. Looking towards the past, I remain a monarchist at heart; looking towards the future I shall become a republican by conviction. And there is one further and perhaps decisive reason for this change. Any attempt at monarchist reaction would now be necessarily linked with the tendency to restore also the archaic militaristic form of the monarchy and of the conservative class-State. The example of the restored Stuarts and Bourbons is repellent. The nation would then be more divided than ever, and the Socialist working masses would never come to accept the restoration. What was true of France after 1871 is true of us today. The Republic is the form of government which divides us least.

Meinecke, *Politische Schriften und Reden*, ed. G. Kotowski. Darmstadt, 1958, pp. 281 ff.

9 The Achievements of the Provisional Government, 1919

FRIEDRICH EBERT

With the meeting of the Weimar Constituent Assembly on 6 February 1919, the German Revolution was formally over. In his address to the Assembly, Friedrich Ebert, who was appointed President of the Republic and remained so until his death in 1925, listed the tasks confronting the Provisional Government on taking office, and described the extent to which it had mastered these difficulties in the subsequent three months. Particularly interesting is Ebert's evocation of that 'other' Germany of Goethe and Schiller, Fichte and 1848, Marx and Lassalle.

Ladies and Gentlemen, the Reich Government expresses its greetings, through me, to the Constituent Assembly of the German Nation. My special greetings go to the women, who appear in the Reich parliament for the first time with equal rights. The Provisional Government owes its mandate to the revolution; it will place it back into the hands of the National Assembly.

(Bravo!)

In the revolution the German people rose up against an old and crumbling tyranny.

(Agreement on the Left: violent protest on the Right.)

As soon as the right of self-determination has been secured for the German people, they will return to the rule of law. Only on the broad road of parliamentary debate and decision-making can the urgently necessary changes, including those in the economic and social field, be realized without destroying the Reich and its economy.

(Very true! Left.)

That is why the Reich Government sees in this National Assembly the supreme and only sovereign in Germany. . . .

We have lost the war. This fact is not a consequence of the revolution.

(Very true! Left: violent protest on the Right.)

Ladies and Gentlemen, it was the Imperial Government of Prince Max of Baden which made arrangements for the armistice which disarmed us.

(Shouts.)

After the collapse of our allies and in view of the military and economic situation there was nothing else it could do.

(Quite right! Left.)

The revolution refused to accept the responsibility for the misery into which the German people were plunged by the mistaken policy of the old régime and the irresponsible over-confidence of the militarists.

(Very true! Left.)

It is also not responsible for our serious food shortage.

(Contradiction, Right.)

Defeat and food shortage have put us at the mercy of the enemy Powers...

...Ladies and Gentlemen, the Provisional Government was faced with a terrible task. We were in the truest sense the trustees in bankruptcy of the old régime.

(Very true! from the Social Democratic benches.)

The future will be hard. But we place our trust nevertheless in the unshakeable creativity of the German nation. The old bases of German power are broken for ever. The Prussian hegemony, the Hohenzollern army, the policy of shining armour, have become impossible for us for all time. Just as 9 November linked up with 18 March 1848 (shouts from the Independent Socialists), so we, here in Weimar, must effect the transition from Imperialism to Idealism, from World Power to spiritual greatness. The Wilhelmine Era, preoccupied only with external brilliance, is well described in Lassalle's words, that classical German thinkers and poets flew over it in crane-like flight. Now the spirit of Weimar, the spirit of the great philosopher and poet, must again fill our lives.

(Shouts from the Independent Socialists: Bravo! from the German Democratic Party.)

So we shall go to work with our grand aim firmly before us, to safe-guard the rights of the German people, to establish a strong democracy in Germany . . . and to fill it with a true Socialist spirit and Socialist action. . . . So we shall achieve what Fichte proclaimed was the task of the German nation: 'We want to erect a Reich of justice and truth, based upon the equality of all human beings'.

(Stormy applause from the Social Democrats and the Left.)

Ritter and Miller, *Die deutsche Revolution*, pp. 193–8.

V

The Foreign Policy
of the Weimar Republic

In his controversial book on the *Origins of the Second World War*,
A. J. P. Taylor asserted that, though Hitler changed many things, 'his
foreign policy was that of his predecessors, of the professional diplomats
at the foreign ministry, and indeed of all Germans'. Most historians
– and many ex-Nazis in Germany – read this as an attempt to exculpate
Hitler. Professor Golo Mann, on the other hand, has pointed to the
'perverse ambiguity' of this view: 'If Hitler pursued the same policy
as Stresemann, then Stresemann pursued the same policy as Hitler;
if Hitler pursued only the normal, the only possible German policy
. . . then conquest and mastery on the Continent was the only possible
German policy.' The issue here is a complex one. Germany was
undoubtedly treated harshly at Versailles. The principle of national
self-determination was applied only where it worked against Germany,
as in the Danish peninsula and in the establishment of the Polish corridor which separated East Prussia from the rest of Germany; it was
ignored where it would have worked in Germany's favour, as in the
case of German Austria, whose population unanimously desired
Anschluss with Germany. The reparations imposed on Germany,
which had its own immense war debts to pay, were recognized by
Keynes as completely unrealistic. On the other hand, Germany remained – potentially – the strongest power in Europe. In 1914, she
had been 'encircled' by the massive strength of Russia, France and
Great Britain. Now Bolshevik Russia was diplomatically isolated
and torn by civil war; on Germany's eastern border was not the
Russian colossus but the weak new Polish state; in the south-east,
the collapse of Germany's allies, Austria-Hungary and Turkey, had
left a vast power-vacuum; France and Britain were exhausted and
had military commitments all over the world which they were unable

to meet; and the United States withdrew into isolation. In this situation, British and French statesmen were in a dilemma. If they made concessions to Germany, she would become rapidly more powerful, and though the aims of her democratic leaders might be relatively limited, there was no guarantee that nationalist forces might not seize power at a later date. If, on the other hand, they kept Germany down, they were playing into the hands of those very nationalist forces and – as Hugo Preuss plaintively cried in 1923 – destroying the already crumbling position of the democrats. In the end they chose the worst possible course – they dealt severely with the democrats and then appeased the most extreme nationalists. It was, as Vansittart said, 'the great mistake of relatively modern history'.

1 The Republic in Danger, 1923

HUGO PREUSS

Looking back on his Constitution in 1923, Preuss admitted that there were numerous internal obstacles to the proper functioning of democracy in Germany, and that the suspicion of foreign powers about the durability of the democratic order was therefore understandable, but he insisted that the greatest obstacle faced by the Republic was the severity with which it was being treated by those very powers.

When the National Assembly in Weimar accepted the new Reich constitution on 31 July 1919, with the overwhelming majority of 262, against only 75 votes of the extreme Left and the Right, the most important precondition for the reorganization of Germany on a national and democratic basis had been created. . . . If the relatively quick and successful acceptance of the constitution raised perhaps too high hopes of its equally quick and successful implementation, then the experience of the past few years has been a bitter disappointment.

As a reflection of this disappointment voices can now be heard which express doubts as to whether the constitution and its national and democratic principles can ever be put into effect. For this implementation presupposes, it is said, a transformation of the national character;

and the possibility of such a transformation is contradicted by historical experience. Despite constitutional changes the basic political character of the English and French people has remained essentially unchanged through the centuries; despite the unparalleled revolution in Russia the Bolsheviks are able to rule there with essentially unchanged Tsarist methods, because this method of government suits the national character. Similarly, the German national character demands an auto-cratic régime – though one as 'enlightened' as possible, and trimmed with modern forms of interest representation; for the German character lacks the necessary precondition of democratic self-government: the unifying force of a national community spirit. And because this is lacking, the principle of the nation-State is being overwhelmed and torn apart by the conflict of economic, religious and social classes and interest groups, and by the particularism of the separate States. The autocratic heritage of the latter is being used as an excuse for allowing them to get on as before with the business of governing, while one goes about one's own unpolitical business unhindered. . . . In this situation the Weimar constitution cannot be implemented; for it is evident that the people, its elected representatives and its political leaders are not even able to operate the apparatus of demo-cratic-parliamentary self-government which the constitution set up. On the contrary they are turning it into a mockery, so that the already weak faith of suspicious foreign countries in the permanency of our new political system is being completely destroyed.

Even he who continues to have faith in the practicability of our new constitution cannot ignore the partial accuracy and grave impli-cations of such criticism. But to be able to assess accurately the inherent strengths and weaknesses of the new political order, one must first weigh the tremendous obstacles which are being put in the path of the new constitution from abroad. The suspicious foreign countries have the least right of all to level such criticism at our internal development; for the most important cause of all those obstacles is the illegal maltreat-ment of the national democracy by the victors over the Prussian Kaiserdom. If the latter was born out of the brilliance of victory, the German Republic was born out of its terrible defeat. This difference in origin cast from the first a dark shadow on the new political order, as far as national sentiment was concerned; but initially the belief still predominated that that new order was necessary for the rebirth of Germany. That is why the democratic clauses of the Weimar constitution met with relatively little resistance, despite the unrivalled severity of the armistice terms. For everyone still expected a peace settlement in accordance with Wilson's fourteen points, which all the belligerent countries had bindingly accepted as the basis for the peace. This would have left the new Germany with the political and economic chance to survive and gradually pull itself up again, instead of turning it into the pariah among European nations by malevolently draining its national life-blood. The criminal madness of the Versailles *Diktat* was a shameless blow in the face to such hopes based on international law and political common sense. The Reich constitution of Weimar was born with this curse upon it. That it did not collapse immediately under the strain is striking proof of the intrinsic vitality of its basic principles; but its implementation and evolution were inevitably fatefully restricted and lamed thereby. If the German people as a whole had immediately recognized at that time all the monstrous implications of this quite impossible peace-less peace – perhaps the elementary drive of self-preservation might have inspired it with the unifying force of desperate resistance. . . .

It is only too easy to understand that sentiments should have arisen in this maltreated nation which provided fertile ground for every agitation against the new political order. The sight of the impotent misery of the Republic made many people forget that Germany was driven into this misery under the old system; the contrast between then and now is so monstrous, terrible and incomprehensible that the voices of blind and bitter passion are easily louder than those of political common sense. And if some flee from the hopeless present into the shadow of the past, others take refuge in heady enthusiasm for mad day dreams which promise to erect a new utopian world on the ruins of all established order. The victorious powers, and France especially, justify their policy of endlessly beating down Germany with the argument that the weakness of the Republic and the strength of its reactionary and nihilistic enemies do not permit confidence to arise in the durability of the new constitutional order; and yet it is precisely this policy which has done everything and left nothing undone to weaken the German Republic and strengthen its enemies by destroying the belief that Germany could resurrect itself on the basis of the new constitution.

Deutschlands Republikanische Reichsverfassung, 2nd edition, Berlin, 1923, pp. 97–102.

2 German Behaviour
at the Spa Conference, 1920
VISCOUNT D'ABERNON

D'Abernon was British ambassador to Germany from 1920 to 1926. His notes on the Spa Conference of July 1920 show why the Allies came to believe that the democratic forces were not in full control of German affairs.

Spa, 5 July 1920. The conference made a bad start today. This is hardly surprising for the German delegation have not been more than a few days in office and have had little time to study their briefs. The consequence was that when they were closely questioned regarding disarmament, their answers were unsatisfactory and went to show that the national thoroughness which the Germans affect is not merely predilection but a physical necessity; without thorough preparations they are apparently lost. It was unfortunate for them that the first issue raised at the conference was the highly technical one of Germany's present state of disarmament; so technical was it that the leading German delegates, after endeavouring to answer without prompting, were obliged to call experts to their assistance, since they professed inability to deal with the problem from their own knowledge. . . .

Spa, 6 July 1920. Today, Herr Gessler, the German Minister of War, and General von Seeckt, the Commander of the Reichswehr, arrived, accompanied by a staff small in number but gigantic in stature. He was immediately called to the conference, and made a dramatic appearance. A rather haughty demeanour and extreme military stiffness – these were in striking contrast with the rather dejected appearance of the German civilians. Von Seeckt is an austere man, with a severe death's-head face and an ultra-correct ceremonious manner. He was supported by two subordinate blond giants. The three wore the sober uniform of the new German Army, with iron crosses and other war medals. The effect produced by their appearance was different on different minds. Lloyd George, who has little sympathy with military pomp and paraphernalia, thought the appearance in uniform a signal instance of military arrogance and tactlessness. Allied soldiers, on the other hand, took the opposite view. . . .

Spa, 12 July 1920. The previous meetings of the conference have been sensational enough, but today all records were surpassed. The sensation was caused by Herr Stinnes, the great coal magnate, who made a most violent outburst at the Supreme Council. I do not know why the official German delegates asked that Stinnes should be heard; they must have known the danger. No sooner had the President invited Herr Stinnes to address the conference, than he rose and read a carefully prepared speech. The studied deliberateness with which he spoke added to the offensiveness of the phraseology. He said 'I rise because I want to look everybody in the face. M. Millerand announced yesterday that we Germans were accorded the right to speak as a matter of courtesy. I claim to speak as a matter of right. Whoever is not afflicted with the disease of victory. . .' At this point Stinnes was stopped by the President. Dr Simons interfered gently with the remark that Herr Stinnes had no official status. Later on when referring to the Allied threat to occupy the Ruhr, Stinnes broke out again, and declared in a roaring voice: 'If black troops – those worthy instruments of Allied policy – are used for this purpose, the feeling of every white man will recoil, nor will the Allies get any coal'.

The Allied delegates were pale with anger and surprise; the Belgian President, M. Delacroix, sharply called the German coal king to order. It was subsequently explained by Dr Simons, with a view to allaying excitement, that Stinnes was in the habit of addressing board meetings in similar tones. M. Hymans, the Belgian Foreign Minister, remarked on this: 'What would have happened to us with such a man, if he had been in the position of the conqueror?'.

An Ambassador of Peace. Hodder and Stoughton, London, 1929, Vol. I, pp. 59–64.

3 War against Poland
and perhaps France, 1919

JOACHIM VON STÜLPNAGEL

Allied suspicions of the intentions of the German army were not entirely without foundation, as is shown in this letter from Stülpnagel, chief of the operations section of the High Command, to General von Seeckt, dated 28 June 1919.

In my opinion it is absolutely essential that an officer corps with monarchical convictions and of the old stamp should be preserved for the miserable creature of the new army. Counter-moves are naturally on the way. I have been informed that *Herr General* [Seeckt] has handed in his resignation. After the decree of the war minister no other step was feasible. . . . I am hoping that within the foreseeable future the resurrection of the monarchy, a struggle with Poland and perhaps with France too will be possible, and I therefore consider it my duty to ask *Herr General* to remain in the army for these tasks and for these aims.

F. L. Carsten, *The Reichswehr and Politics 1918–33*. Oxford University Press, 1966, pp. 30.

4 Germany and Russia, 1922

HANS VON SEECKT

As head of the Army Command 1920–6, Seeckt was one of the most powerful men in Germany; he came close, on several occasions, to establishing a military dictatorship. During the First World War he had demanded the creation of a line of German satellite States stretching from the Atlantic to Persia. On 11 September 1922, he outlined what F. L. Carsten has called the 'basic idea' of his foreign policy: the partition of Poland between Germany and the Soviet Union.

Poland's existence is intolerable, incompatible with the survival of Germany. It must disappear, and it will disappear through its own internal weakness and through Russia – with our assistance. For Russia Poland is even more intolerable than for us; no Russia can allow Poland to exist. With Poland falls one of the strongest pillars of the Treaty of Versailles, the preponderance of France.... Poland can never offer any advantage to Germany, either economically, because it is incapable of any development, or politically, because it is France's vassal. The re-establishment of the broad common frontier between Russia and Germany is the precondition for the regaining of strength of both countries. 'Russia and Germany within the frontiers of 1914!' should be the basis of reaching an understanding between the two....

We aim at two things: first, a strengthening of Russia in the economic and the political, thus also in the military field, and so indirectly a strengthening of ourselves, by strengthening a possible ally of the future; we further desire, at first cautiously and experimentally, a direct strengthening of ourselves, by helping to create in Russia an armaments industry which in case of need will serve us....

In all these enterprises, which to a large extent are only beginning, the participation and even the official knowledge of the German government must be entirely excluded. The details of the negotiations must remain in the hands of the military authorities.

F. L. Carsten, *The Reichswehr and Politics 1918–33*, pp. 140–1.

5 Germany's Failure to Disarm, 1925

J. H. MORGAN

Brigadier-General Morgan was the leading British member of the Allied Commission of Control for the Disarmament of Germany from 1919 to 1923. The son of a German Swiss mother, he quickly became convinced that the Republic had no hope of survival. In November 1923 he predicted the rise of 'some great military adventurer of German blood' who would 'sweep like an avalanche across the West'. In a letter of 31 January 1925 to the German pacifist, F. W. Foerster, General Morgan gave the reasons for his continuing distrust of Germany.

. . . Let me try at the outset to put the Allied case in the form of a few plain questions. And first, why does the Reichswehrministerium persistently refuse to disclose its recruiting returns, the Mannschaftsuntersuchungslisten and Annahmebücher. These alone can establish how many men are being called up for training by the *Reichsheer* [*sic*] (Regular Army), and for five years they have been constantly refused. Why? The reason given is that they are a matter of 'inner service' which does not concern us. But is it no concern of ours to know how many men are being trained to the use of arms? And if there is nothing to conceal, why conceal it?

In the second place, why does the Reichswehrministerium refuse to show us those registers of armament production which were snatched away from under our very noses at Spandau? They alone can serve to establish what your gun establishment was in 1919 and what it is now.

Thirdly, why does the Reichswehrministerium insist on retaining control of the vast network of military establishments, artillery depots, munition depots, supply depots, remount depots, which supplied the needs of the old army and are altogether superfluous for the needs, the legitimate needs, of the new? Your government does not expropriate these, it does not alienate them, it does not sell them, it does not convert them – it either leaves them idle or lets them to a tenant at will. They are available for the mobilization of a vast army at almost any moment. A trifling sum of 200,000 gold marks is all that appears in the Reichshaushaltsplan (the Budget) for 1924 as the proceeds of a sale of some two or three of them. What is being done with all the rest?

Fourthly, why is the Reichswehrministerium paying no less than twenty-two officers in the Ministry alone, without taking account of the generals in the Wehrkreis commands, as lieutenant-generals and major-generals? Why are all the captains in the Reichsheer with over two years' service drawing the pay of majors, and the oberleutnants drawing the pay of captains? Why is your government maintaining an establishment of Feldwebels and Unteroffiziers sufficient for an army thrice, and more than thrice, the Treaty strength? To a soldier there is only one explanation of these things and that is that this army is, and is destined to be, a cadre for expansion.

What of your 'Security Police'? The questions whether they should live in barracks or out of barracks, whether they should be organized in Hundertschaften (centuries) or not so organized, whether every twenty men should be armed with more than one machine-gun – all these are minor questions compared with the profoundly significant fact that they are, by one statute after another, made interchangeable with the Reichsheer in pay, promotion, pensions, grades and a dozen other things, so that the two forces match one another even as the wards of a lock match the key which fits it. Behind every Reichsheer soldier their stands, like a silhouette, a 'police official'.

As to your army expenditure – and I have studied your budget – I will only say this: if your army is really as small as your government say it is, then your government is the most extravagant government in the world; and if your government is not extravagant, then your army is far larger than it ought to be. Your Reichsheer, in theory small in stature, projects in reality a gigantic shadow across the map of Germany, and the shadow is the greater reality of the two. That shadow is the old army. Everything that an ingenious brain could devise and a subtle intellect invent, down even to giving the companies of infantry of the new army the numbers and badges of the regiments of the old, has been done to ensure that, at a touch of a button, the new army shall expand to the full stature of its predecessor. The proofs in my possession are overwhelming.

Your government tell us repeatedly that our work is done and that there is nothing left to find out. They tell us that the Treaty of Versailles has been loyally executed. How then do they explain the astounding paradox that every time a store of hidden arms in a factory is revealed to the Commission by a pacifist workman, the workman, if discovered, is immediately arrested and sentenced to a long term of penal servitude? There have been scores of such cases, and I am told that the unhappy German workman, who only the other day disclosed to us the great stores of arms in Berlin, is the latest, but I fear he will not be the last, of the victims. If, as your Reichswehrministerium informed the Commission when disputing the necessity of an enactment by the Reichstag to abolish compulsory service, the military clauses of the Treaty 'are part of the law of Germany', these unfortunate workmen were merely assisting in the execution of the law. If these concealments of arms are not approved by the German Government, why are the workmen who disclose them ruthlessly punished and the factory owners who conceal them allowed to go free?

Assize of Arms, 2 Vols. Methuen, 1945, Vol. I, pp. 268–70.

6 The Ultimate Aim, 1926

JOACHIM VON STÜLPNAGEL

What was the ultimate objective of the German army leaders in the Weimar period? This memorandum of 6 March 1926, approved by Seeckt and sent by Stülpnagel to the German Foreign Office, lists aims which bear a striking resemblance to those pursued both before 1918 and after 1933.

The immediate aim of German policy must be the regaining of full sovereignty over the area retained by Germany, the firm acquisition of those areas at present separated from her, and the re-acquisition of those areas essential to the German economy. That is to say:

1. The liberation of the Rhineland and the Saar area.
2. The abolition of the Corridor and the regaining of Polish Upper Silesia.
3. The *Anschluss* of German Austria.
4. The abolition of the Demilitarized Zone.

These immediate political aims will produce conflict primarily with France and Belgium and with Poland which is dependent on them, then with Czechoslovakia and finally also with Italy. . . .

The above exposition of Germany's political aims . . . clearly shows that the problem for Germany in the next stages of her political development can only be the re-establishment of her position in Europe, and that the regaining of her world position will be a task for the distant future. Re-establishing a European position is for Germany a question in which land forces will almost exclusively be decisive, for the opponent of this resurrection of Germany is in the first place France. It is certainly to be assumed that a reborn Germany will eventually come into conflict with the American–English powers in the struggle for raw materials and markets, and that she will then need adequate maritime forces. But this conflict will be fought out on the basis of a firm European position, after a new solution to the Franco–German problem has been achieved through either peace or war.

Akten zur Deutschen Auswärtigen Politik, 1918–1945, Serie B: 1925–33, Vol. I, 1, Göttingen, 1966, pp. 343–5.

7 Stresemann's Foreign Aims, 1925

GUSTAV STRESEMANN

How did the aims of Stresemann, Germany's Foreign Minister from 1923 to 1929, differ from those of Seeckt? In 1925, Stresemann signed the Locarno Pact with France accepting Germany's territorial losses in the west but leaving the eastern border problem open. For this, as for his agreement that Germany should join the League of Nations, he was violently attacked by nationalist forces in Germany. In actual fact, however, Stresemann had a number of territorial ambitions in east and south-east Europe. In January 1925 he defined his 'immediate aim' as the restoration of the 1914 frontier in the east, and his 'distant aim' as the incorporation into Germany of all German-speaking areas in central Europe. He returned to this question in a famous letter of 7 September 1925 to the ex-Crown Prince.

On the question of Germany's entry into the League I would make the following observations:

In my opinion there are three great tasks that confront German foreign policy in the more immediate future –

In the first place the solution of the Reparations question in a sense tolerable for Germany, and the assurance of peace, which is an essential premise for the recovery of our strength.

Secondly, the protection of Germans abroad, those 10 to 12 millions of our kindred who now live under a foreign yoke in foreign lands.

The third great task is the readjustment of our eastern frontiers; the recovery of Danzig, the Polish corridor, and a correction of the frontier in Upper Silesia.

In the background stands the union with German Austria, although I am quite clear that this not merely brings no advantages to Germany, but seriously complicates the problem of the German Reich.

If we want to secure these aims, we must concentrate on these tasks. Hence the Security Pact, which guarantees us peace and constitutes England, as well as Italy, if Mussolini consents to collaborate, as guarantors of our western frontiers. The pact also rules out the possibility of any military conflict with France for the recovery of

Alsace-Lorraine; this is a renunciation on the part of Germany, but, in so far, it possesses only a theoretic character, as there is no possibility of a war against France. . . .

The question of a choice between east and west does not arise as the result of our joining the League. Such a choice can only be made when backed by military force. That, alas we do not possess. We can neither become a continental spear-head for England, as some believe, nor can we involve ourselves in an alliance with Russia. I would utter warning against any utopian ideas of coquetting with Bolshevism. When the Russians are in Berlin, the red flag will at once be flown from the castle, and in Russia, where they hope for a world revolution, there will be much joy at the Bolshevization of Europe as far as the Elbe; the rest of Germany will be thrown to the French to devour. That we are perfectly ready to come to an understanding with the Russian State, in whose evolutionary development I believe, on another basis, and my contention that we are not selling ourselves to the west by joining the League, is a matter on which I would gladly enlarge to Your Royal Highness in a personal talk. The great movement now stirring all the primitive peoples against the colonial domination of the great nations, will in no way be influenced to the disadvantage of these peoples by our joining the League. The most important thing for the first task of German policy mentioned above is, the liberation of German soil from any occupying force. We must get the stranglehold off our neck. On that account, German policy, as Metternich said of Austria, no doubt after 1809, will be one of finesse and the avoidance of great decisions.

I beg Y.R.H. to allow me to confine myself to these brief indications, and I would also ask you kindly to view this letter in the light of the fact that I am compelled to use the greatest reserve in everything I say. If Y.R.H. could give me the opportunity for a quiet talk about these matters that will soon come up urgently for decision, I am gladly available at any time.

Gustav Stresemann, His Diaries, Letters and Papers, edited and translated by Eric Sutton, 3 Vols. Macmillan, 1937, Vol. II, pp. 503–5.

8 Locarno and Potsdam, 1927

F. W. FOERSTER

On 8 December 1927, Foerster made a despairing attempt to persuade Stresemann to dissociate himself from the aims of Prussian militarism.

For thirty years I have been fighting against Prussian nationalism and militarism. . . . As you will see from my *Political Ethics*, which I permit myself to enclose, I have always recognized the valuable traditions and moral forces within that military tradition, but have tried, precisely for this reason, to separate these from their tragic connection with the profoundly anti-social and anti-State daemonic elements of moral anarchy which have been preserved in the Prussian State, itself founded on the ground colonized through constant warfare and conquest by the German order of knights.

I regard myself as one of the most German of all Germans, one who is trying to revive a tradition which has long disappeared from view, but which stems from the deepest recognition of the realities of our European position. . . . I have striven to make this the basis of German political thought and action. If I seem to be attacking your policy . . . it is because of my unswerving attempt to subordinate the power of Prussia to the German character and the German rôle in Europe, rather than allowing those most un-German elements in Germany always to sabotage the execution of a truly consistent and united *German* policy. . . .

I have not the slightest doubt – nor have any of those who really know this caste and the balance of political forces within Germany – that they, in their drive to seize power yet again, will have the aid of inexhaustible material resources, weapons, the traditions of wielding power and the ideology which accompany them. They will further be assisted by three centuries of standing to attention and goose-stepping in Germany. Their ultimate triumph is a foregone conclusion – *unless* men at home and abroad recognize the peril in time and do everything possible to show these groups that their antics will not be tolerated.

That my activity is described by some blinded people as treason will not cause me to change course. My soul is too full of the burning need to save our people and Europe from another catastrophe to bother about the false judgements of those who have been misled. I willingly sacrifice my good name in such a cause.

You, Herr Reichsminister, have described my attempts to speak the truth not only as 'harmful to German interests' but as treason to the cause of European understanding. To this I now wish to answer as follows: I am a German who, on the basis of numerous . . . confidential contacts, probably has closer links with all kinds of foreign people than any of my compatriots. And I can assure you: even without our sounding the alarm . . . the countless parades, declarations and shifts in power in Germany . . . have produced an ever-growing distrust, even in Left-wing circles, of the *aims of the German Right* and the *ability of the German Left* and the German Government to stop the Right from realizing its aims. . . . It is precisely because of this that the foreign policy of our neighbours is no longer able simply to ignore the reality of that other Germany, which sees in Geneva and Locarno only a temporary opportunistic means of restoring German power. . . . I have been meaning to write to you, Herr Reichsminister, for some months now to tell you quite frankly about this crisis of confidence and the only way of overcoming it. To my sorrow I saw that the official representatives of Germany . . . were making the mistake not only of failing to realize for themselves but of denying to foreigners the very existence in our Fatherland of that unteachable nationalist minority, with its vastly superior sources of material and ideological power. This, more than anything, has increased the distrust and aroused suspicion of secret complicity. There is, in this situation, no other way of creating true confidence than to turn the German nation . . . . radically away from these machinations. . . and show it that this is a choice between *either or*, and that one cannot simultaneously support both Locarno and Potsdam without slowly but surely undermining world confidence in Germany. And secondly, those Germans who are honest and ready for compromise must be firm in showing those really unteachable people their power, instead of continually giving the impression that they would not offend those circles for anything in the world.

Stresemann Papers, Foreign and Commonwealth Office Library, London, 7372/H166814–18.

9 The Great Mistake of Modern History, 1939

SIR ROBERT VANSITTART

In May 1939, the Liberal peer Lord Lothian, until Munich one of the staunchest champions of appeasement, wrote to Vansittart at the Foreign Office: 'If we had tried appeasement more vigorously in the days of the Republic there might never have been a Hitler at all.' In his reply, Vansittart, one of Hitler's most determined opponents in this country, expressed whole-hearted agreement.

How different things would have been if we had all provided the Republican régime in Germany with greater concessions and so with greater authority and credit. We might all have lived happily ever afterwards. That of course has been the great mistake of relatively modern history, and I think you and I have always been agreed about that. I shall always regret that throughout the period when that mistaken policy was being followed I was head of the American Department, though I regret the long experience on no other ground!

J. R. M. Butler, *Lord Lothian*. Macmillan, 1960, p. 228.

VI

The Resistible Rise
of Adolf Hitler

Ought Hitler's seizure of power on 30 January 1933 to be interpreted as a revolution, a restoration, or a synthesis between the two? A photo-montage by Heartfield on Hitler's claim that 'millions stand behind me' shows a faceless businessman putting 'millions' of marks into Hitler's upraised hand. This Marxist view of Hitler merely as a counter-revolutionary does not take into account the fact that Hitler *was* supported not only by millions of marks but also by millions of Germans. To many of the aristocrats who invited him into power he was little better than a Bolshevik, even after his elimination in the bloody *coup* of 30 June 1934 of his own 'revolutionary' wing. Hitler and his henchmen mostly came from the gutter; the massive electoral following which they achieved was taken primarily from the middle-class Liberal parties, and not from the Communists, Social Democrats, Catholics or Conservative aristocrats. When the Nazis lost some two million votes at the second Reichstag election of 1932, Goebbels for one thought that everything was lost. Two other factors now played into Hitler's hands. The first, which had been noticeable since 1930, was the almost indecent readiness of the democratic parties to abandon responsibility. The second, and more important, was the totally unrealistic aim of Papen and Schleicher of setting up an authoritarian régime 'above the parties'. They finally vied with one another to win Hitler's millions for their schemes, only to find that Hitler, once in office, was less easily controlled than they had imagined.

1 The White General, 1919

GEORGE GROSZ

Rosa Luxemburg and Karl Liebknecht, the two Spartacist (Communist) leaders, were murdered by Free Corps officers in January 1919. This drawing of 'The White General' by the famous Left-wing artist George Grosz (who emigrated to the U.S.A. in 1933 and was deprived of his citizenship by Hitler) was made in 1919: it shows an officer of the Free Corps already wearing the Swastika.

2 The Assassination at Speyer 1924

ERNST VON SALOMON

Political murder was something new in German history, a product of the
First World War. The Centre party leader Matthias Erzberger was assas-
sinated in 1921, the liberal industrialist Walther Rathenau in 1922. Ernst
von Salomon, who was imprisoned for his part in Rathenau's murder, pub-
lished an anthology in 1934 to illustrate the work of the Free Corps. His
volume included the following passage on the assassination of the separatist
government of the Palatinate. It shows the mentality of the men who later
joined the S.A. and the S.S.

Captain Ehrhardt gave the following orders:

'Right, Fritz, the separatist government of the Palatinate is to be
shot tomorrow night. . . . Will you do the job? I want your answer
in half an hour.' 'I need no time for reflection, Herr Kapitän, I'll see
to it! . . .' A forceful handshake and I was dismissed. At the door he
called me back: 'One more thing, Fritz, if you get into a fight with
the rabble or the French, keep the last bullet for yourself. Don't fall
into the hands of that pack of swine, understand?' Every word was
short and abrupt and emphasized by a pronounced nod of the head.
He raised his arm at an angle to shoulder height. At the words 'pack
of swine' his clenched fist delivered a knock-out blow to an invisible
enemy! That was the 'old man' all over, grisly and curt with none of
this humanitarian rubbish. . . .

Everything went well. We got into 'enemy territory' without arousing
suspicion. Of course the Negroes and Zouaves provoked our anger.
But my anger was never so great as when I saw the separatist mob
in the streets of Ludwigshafen. So these were the 'soldiers' of the
autonomous Palatinate! The most degenerate pack that one could
imagine. . . .

We had agreed to assemble at a small inn in Speyer. It was essential
to keep everybody under surveillance. The failure of one man, and
both our plan and our lives would be in danger. . . . Leibrecht and I
saw to it that everyone ate a hearty supper and did not drink too
much. . . .

Shortly before half-past nine the messenger from the group in the dining room arrived, bringing me a paper serviette on which was clearly indicated the table occupied by Heinz Orbis and his loyal followers. I was also told that one non-participant was sitting at the same table. I regretted that I could make no allowances for him. . . .

Our aim was the second table on the right behind the Spanish wall in the dining room. . . . I was ticking over like clockwork. I had suppressed every emotion. We entered the dining room without haste. I kept my hat on. . . . Why bother with courtesy when we had very special greetings to deliver on behalf of an enslaved nation. . . . My aim is that man there in the green hunting suit, the one with the red pointed beard, the devil personified, the man who had caused such suffering and misery to thousands of his fellow countrymen and disgracefully betrayed his Fatherland. I wipe my forehead with the handkerchief in my left hand, the prearranged signal. . . . Weinmann jumps up, trying to pull out his pistol and shout: 'Hands up, we are interested only in the separatists!' I just have time to see his weapon has caught in his jacket pocket, he is standing there pulling and shouting 'Ha . . . Ha . . .' I can't wait any longer. With one leap I'm standing beside Herr Orbis. . . . As Weinmann begins to shout I pull the trigger twice. Two more shots hit the man on my right, and another gets the third man. I see him trying to shout, he is the non-participant. He got a bullet right through the mouth and is still counting his good fortune. I glance round at Heinz Orbis, who in one final effort has got up and is stumbling towards the back door. A shot in the back brings him crashing down.

Harry Pross, *Die Zerstörung der deutschen Politik*. Fischer, 1959, pp. 82–3.

3 The Kapp Putsch, 1920

WOLFGANG KAPP

In March 1920, General Lüttwitz and a retired civil servant, Kapp, one of the founders of the Fatherland Party of 1917, marched into Berlin at the head of Captain Ehrhardt's Free Corps brigade (wearing the Swastika) and tried to establish a conservative régime. The operation failed when the Republican government left for Stuttgart and the trade unions called a general strike. Kapp's proclamation of 13 March 1920 revealed his intentions.

The Reich and nation are in grave danger. With terrible speed we are approaching the complete collapse of the State and of law and order. The people are only dimly aware of the approaching disaster. Prices are rising unchecked. Hardship is growing. Starvation threatens. Corruption, usury, nepotism and crime are cheekily raising their heads. The government, lacking in authority, impotent, and in league with corruption, is incapable of overcoming the danger. Away with a government in which Erzberger is the leading light!

From the east we are threatened by destruction and violation by war-like Bolshevism. Is this government capable of resisting it? How are we to escape internal and external collapse?

Only by re-erecting a strong State. What principles should be our guide?

Not reaction, but a free development of the German State, restoration of order and the sanctity of the law. Duty and conscience must reign again in the German land. German honour and honesty must be restored. . . .

The hour of the salvation of Germany is at hand and must be used; therefore there is no other way but a government of action.

What are the tasks facing this new government?

The government will

carry out the terms of the Peace Treaty while safeguarding the honour of the German nation . . . as far as this is possible without leading to self-destruction . . .

The government will

ruthlessly suppress strikes and sabotage. Everyone should go peacefully about his work. Everyone willing to work is assured of our firm protection: striking is treason to the nation, the Fatherland and the future.

The government will

... not be a one-sided capitalist one. It will rather save German work from the hard fate of slavery to international big business and hopes by such measures to put an end to the hostility of the working classes to the State ...

The government will

restore rights to those civil servants of all ranks who have suffered since the November days.... In return it demands of its civil servants the old spirit of loyal fulfilment of duty in the service of the general welfare.

The government will

regard it as its most sacred duty to safeguard fully the well-earned pensions of the war-wounded and the families of fallen warriors ...

The government will

secure the freedom of the churches and restore national and religious education in schools.

Attempts to separate from the Reich will be treated as high treason and dealt with by martial law. We are strong enough not to begin our rule with arrests and other violent measures. But we shall suppress with ruthless severity any attempts to rise against the new order.

We shall govern not according to theories but according to the practical needs of the State and the nation as a whole. In the best German tradition the State must stand above the conflict of classes and parties. It is the objective arbiter in the present conflict between capital and labour. We reject the granting of class-advantage either to the Right or the Left. We recognize only German citizens. Every German citizen who in this difficult hour gives to the Fatherland the things that are the Fatherland's, can depend upon us.

Everyone must do his duty! The first duty of every man today is to work. Germany must be a moral working community! The colours of the German Republic are
Black–White–Red!

The Reich Chancellor
Kapp

J. Erger, *Der Kapp-Lüttwitz-Putsch*. Droste Verlag, Düsseldorf, 1967, pp. 324–6.

4 The Kaiser and the Kapp Putsch, 1920
SIGURD VON ILSEMANN

The Kaiser's adjutant recorded the exiled monarch's reactions to the Putsch.

15 March 1920. The Kapp Putsch! Count Bentinck told us of the *coup* in Germany the day before yesterday, as I was walking with the Kaiser in the garden. The Kaiser was completely surprised and grasped my hand in excitement and joy. As in the war, whenever news came of a victory, he said: 'Tonight we shall have champagne'.

22 March 1920. The Kapp-Lüttwitz government has fallen already. A sorry end to this first attempt at reaction. The incident proves that it is much too early to think of restoring a monarchy in Germany, and that, when the time comes, the Kaiser and the Crown Prince will have little chance. South Germany would hardly accept a Hohenzollern. The Kaiser, however, refuses to admit defeat. He still sees it in a favourable light, although we are keeping him fully informed of events. At heart he really cannot have any further doubts; he is merely trying to hide his great disappointment from others. Several times recently he has exclaimed: 'All those people at home are too soft. All it needs is a little pressure and the government will topple and the old system be restored.' We told the Kaiser repeatedly that all steps of this kind would be premature and harmful to the cause.

Der Kaiser in Holland. Biederstein Verlag, Munich, 1967, Vol. I, p. 149.

5 The Great Inflation, 1923

The following table shows the depreciation of the foreign exchange value of the Mark from 1920–3.

January 1913	1·0
January 1920	15·4
July 1920	9·4
January 1921	15·4
July 1921	18·3
January 1922	45·7
July 1922	117·0
January 1923	4,279·0
July 1923	84,150·0
August 1923	1,100,100·0
September 1923	23,540,000·0
October 1923	6,014,300,000·0
November 15 1923	1,000,000,000,000·0

Gustav Stolper, *The German Economy, 1870 to the Present*. Weidenfeld and Nicolson, 1967, p. 84.

6 Seeckt's 'Government Programme', 1923

HANS VON SEECKT

As the inflation reached its height, Seeckt seemed ready to attempt the establishment of a military dictatorship. In October 1923, he drew up a programme on foreign and internal policy.

The special situation of the Reich, internally and externally, demands special methods. . . . Refusal of entry into the League of Nations. Refusal of any new obligation, beyond the stipulations of the Treaty of Versailles, also with regard to the Rhineland. . . . Intensification of the economic and military–political relations with Russia. Refusal of any, even an economic, *rapprochement* with Poland. To extend the economic *rapprochement* with Russia will be an endeavour of the government because it is convinced that both powers depend upon each other. . . . Suppression of all tendencies directed against the existence of the Reich and against the legitimate authority of the Reich and the State, through the use of the means of power of the Reich. Change of the constitution in a federal sense. Formation of a chamber of estates, with elected representatives of the professions and occupations. . . . Combination of the offices of chancellor and prime minister of Prussia. . . . Prohibition of cartels and trusts. Cancellation of collective labour agreements. The trade unions to be replaced by occupational chambers.

F. L. Carsten, *The Reichswehr and Politics 1918–33*, p. 167.

7 Hitler's Views on Privilege

ADOLF HITLER

In the event it was not Seeckt but Hitler who tried, unsuccessfully, to use the discontent caused by inflation to establish a nationalist dictatorship. This passage from Hitler's Table Talk of 1942 clearly shows what separated Hitler from the German National People's Party which aimed at restoring the monarchy.

27 January 1942

The English have to settle certain social problems which are ripe to be settled. At present these problems can still be solved from above, in a reasonable manner. I tremble for them if they don't do it now. For if it's left to the people to take the initiative, the road is open to madness and destruction. Men like Mosley would have had no difficulty in solving the problem, by finding a compromise between Conservatism and Socialism, by opening the road to the masses but without depriving the élite of their rights.

Class prejudices can't be maintained in a socially advanced State like ours, in which the proletariat produces men of such superiority. Every reasonably conducted organization is bound to favour the development of beings of worth. It has been my wish that the educative organizations of the Party should enable the poorest child to lay claim to the highest functions, if he has enough talent. . . . It's essential that a balance should be struck, in such a way that dyed-in-the-wool Conservatives may be abolished as well as Jewish and Bolshevik anarchists. . . .

National Socialism has introduced into daily life the idea that one should choose an occupation because one is predisposed to it by one's aptitudes, and not because one is predestined for it by birth. Thus National Socialism exercises a calming effect. It reconciles men instead of setting them against one another. It's ridiculous that a child should ever feel obliged to take up his father's profession. Only his aptitudes and gifts should be taken into consideration. Why shouldn't a child have propensities that his parents didn't have? Isn't everyone in Germany sprung from the peasantry? One must not put a curb on individuals. On the contrary, one must avoid whatever might prevent them from rising. If one systematically encourages the selection of the fittest, the time will come when talents will again be, in a sort of way, the privilege of an élite.

H. R. Trevor-Roper (ed), *Hitler's Table Talk*. Weidenfeld and Nicolson, 1953, pp. 254–6.

8 The Rise of the Nazi Party, 1930

COUNT HARRY KESSLER

From 1924 to the Wall Street Crash of 1929, the German Republic enjoyed a period of relative stability. The Nazi Party, which had received 32 seats in the Reichstag elections of May 1924, was reduced to 14 seats in December of that year, and 12 in the elections of 1928. In his diary, Count Kessler, friend and biographer of Walther Rathenau, recorded his dismay at the success of the Nazis in the election of September 1930.

15 September 1930

A black day for Germany. At about four o'clock I received a telegram from Guseck with the election results. The Nazis have increased their representation tenfold, they have risen from 12 to 107 seats and have thus become the second largest party in the Reichstag. The impression abroad is bound to be catastrophic, the aftermath, both diplomatically and financially, will be dreadful. With 107 Nazis, 41 Hugenbergers, and over 70 Communists, that is to say some 220 deputies who radically reject the present German State and seek to overthrow it by revolutionary means, we are confronted with a political crisis which can only be mastered by the formation of a strong united front of all those forces which support or at least tolerate the Republic. . . . In fact, the next move *must* be (*if* there isn't a *Putsch*) the formation of a 'Grand Coalition' between the present governing parties and the Social Democrats. as otherwise government will simply come to a halt. A disturbing detail is the failure of the State Party (Democrats), which gained only 20 seats, that is, less than the Democrats had in the previous Reichstag – despite the alliance with the Young German Order. The German bourgeoisie (represented by the State Party and the People's Party) seems to be on its deathbed, politically. . . .

National Socialism is the feverish symptom of the dying German petty bourgeoisie; but the poison of its illness can bring misery to Germany and Europe for decades to come. This class cannot be saved; but in its death-throes it can bring terrible new suffering to Europe.

Harry Graf Kessler, *Tagebücher 1918–37*. Insel-Verlag, Frankfurt a.M., 1961, pp. 640–1.

9 Unemployment and the Rise of National Socialism

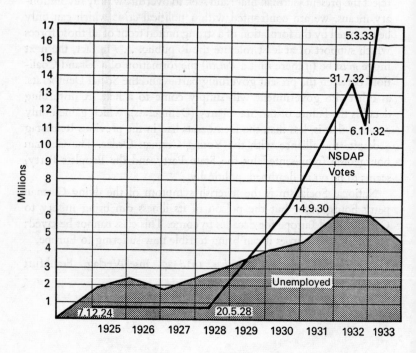

10 Who lost votes to the Nazis?

These two tables show that the Nazis made their massive gains largely at the expense of the Protestant middle classes, who had previously voted for the DNVP, DVP and DDP.

(a) COMPOSITION OF THE GERMAN REICHSTAG

Parties	1919	1921	May 1924	Dec. 1924	1928	1930	July 1932	Nov. 1932	1933
NSDAP (Nazi)	—	—	32	14	12	107	230	196	288
DNVP (Cons.)	44	71	95	103	73	41	37	51	52
DVP (Nat. Lib.)	19	65	45	51	45	31	7	11	2
Wirtschaftspartei	4	4	10	17	31	23	2	1	—
Splinter groups of Right	3	5	19	12	20	55	9	12	7
BVP (Bavarian Cath.)	18	21	16	19	16	19	22	20	18
Centre (Catholics)	73	64	65	69	62	68	75	70	74
DDP (Democrats)	75	39	28	32	25	20	4	2	5
SPD (Soc. Dems.)	163	102	100	131	153	143	133	121	120
USPD (Indep. Socs.)	22	84	—	—	—	—	—	—	—
KPD (Communists)	—	4	62	45	54	77	89	100	81
Total	421	459	472	493	491	583	608	584	647

Gerhart Binder, *Epoche der Entscheidungen*. Stuttgart, 1960, p. 155

(b) VOTES (IN MILLIONS) AT GENERAL ELECTIONS, 1924–32

Parties	1924	1928	1930	July 1932	Nov. 1932
Working class parties (Social Democrats and Communists)	10·5	12·3	13·0	13·1	13·1
Middle class parties (excluding Centre party)	13·2	12·9	10·3	4·0	5·3
Catholic Centre Party	4·1	3·7	4·1	4·5	4·2
National Socialists	0·9	0·8	6·4	13·7	11·7

G. Barraclough, *Factors in German History*. Blackwell, 1946, pp. 147–8.

11 The Electoral Support of the Nazi Party

K. D. BRACHER

... This development was doubly significant because the coming of the economic crisis and the growth of unemployment after 1929 introduced an element of social unrest into town and countryside which, as in 1923, enabled radical propaganda, and especially Right-wing extremism, to book sudden and concrete political successes. Even the communal and diet elections of 1929 revealed everywhere a shift in the balance of forces primarily to the advantage of the National Socialists, and only in second place to the advantage of Communist radicalism. The breeding ground of these plebiscitary movements was the lesser peasantry and also those white-collar and petty bourgeois classes in whom the fear of sinking into the proletariat ... led to violent reactions. Perceptive analyses of the social structure established even at that time how much more important this fact was than the ... idea of class conflict between capitalism and socialism, with which vulgar Marxists tried to explain the rise of 'fascism'. All the regional studies undertaken so far prove that the rise of National Socialism occurred less in areas where there was a sharp class conflict between, for example, larger farmers and agrarian proletariat, and more in agricultural areas with a lesser peasantry, and in town areas with a petty bourgeois population.

However, this sociological explanation is inadequate. It is well-known how much the support of National Socialism by the deluded Hugenberg group, so powerful in industry and the press, contributed to Hitler's penetration into new spheres of influence. In this way, men who had till then not been taken seriously were made socially acceptable, and the German Nationalist Party joined with the National Socialists in forming a 'National Opposition' ... which aimed from autumn 1929 onwards to bring about the final destruction of parliamentary democracy....

The Reichstag elections of 14 September 1930, necessitated by Brüning's fateful decision to dissolve the parliament prematurely, are rightly seen as an event of historic importance. With more than 18 per cent of the votes the NSDAP could increase its number of seats nine-fold. Only the KPD could continue the rise it had already begun, though to a much lesser extent, and only the Centre Party now remained stable. All other parties suffered heavy losses. . . .

The main centres of National Socialist electoral success, which suddenly transformed a small group of extremists into the second largest party after the SPD, were – and were to remain – the agrarian and partly also petty bourgeois areas with a Protestant population. Electorally, as in other respects, the strongest and most persistent resistance to the rise of National Socialism came either from the solidly Catholic or the strongly industrialized areas. The top National Socialist constituency was Schleswig-Holstein, which in summer 1932 was the only German *Land* to show an absolute majority of 51 per cent for the NSDAP; then came Chemnitz-Zwickau, Pomerania, East Hanover, Frankfurt-on-Oder, the Palatinate, Liegnitz and Hesse-Nassau, that is, predominantly Protestant and agricultural constituencies. On the other hand 10 of the 11 constituencies which showed the lowest National Socialist vote in these final years were Catholic. In Cologne-Aachen the National Socialists hardly surpassed 17 per cent even in 1932, and not many more electors chose Hitler in Lower and Upper Bavaria (which had hitherto been so susceptible), in Westphalia and in Berlin. Further statistical analysis would show how important regional, sociological and confessional differences were – a fact which is quite clear also in the numerous elections of the final two years. Suffice it to say that the top seven National Socialist constituencies lay in North Germany, that they were almost without exception close to the frontiers of Germany (proof of the effectiveness of National Socialist revisionist propaganda), but that Catholic constituencies remained more resistant, even where they were close to the frontier and had an agrarian social structure. And although the agrarian component of this militant nationalism was thus extremely prominent, such agrarian constituencies as Oppeln, Upper and Lower Bavaria, and Württemberg proved to be among the most stable.

Deutschland zwischen Demokratie und Diktatur. Bern/Munich, 1964, pp. 73–6.

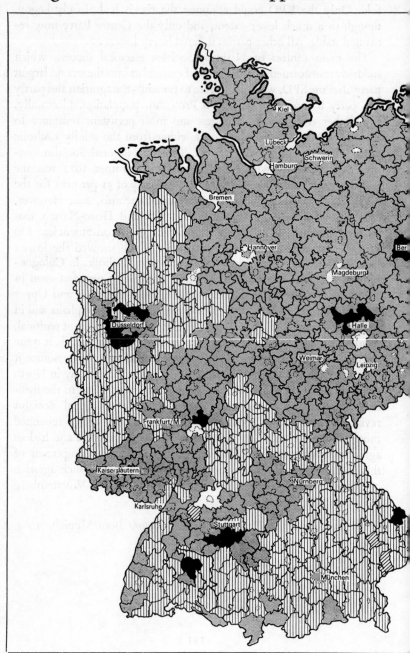

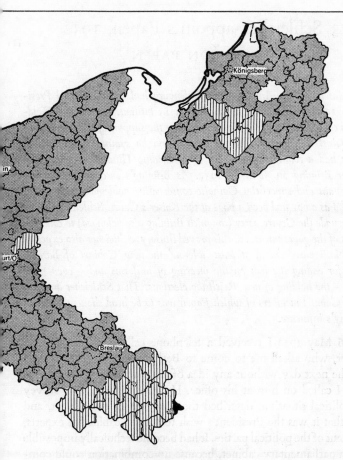

**The Reichstag election of
6th. November 1932**

Constituencies in which
parties gained a majority

 N.S.D.A.P.

Centre or B.V.P.

S.P.D.

K.P.D.

Peasant Party

13 Schleicher appoints Papen, 1932

FRANZ VON PAPEN

On 13 March and 10 April 1932, Hindenburg had been re-elected President with 19 million votes against Hitler's 13 million, but the old Field-Marshal's conscience troubled him for accepting the support of the Republican parties against the 'national' forces with whom he sympathized. General Schleicher had a relatively easy task in persuading Hindenburg to dismiss Chancellor Brüning on 30 May 1932. As Brüning's successor, Schleicher chose the vain and superficial Catholic conservative nobleman, Franz von Papen, who as a boy had been a page at the Kaiser's Court. Schleicher's hope was to persuade the Centre party (to which Brüning also belonged) to continue its support of the government, but this proved illusory. Schleicher also expected that the Nazi party would at least 'tolerate' the new 'Cabinet of Barons' in return for ending the ban on the wearing of uniforms and – even more important – the holding of new Reichstag elections. That Schleicher drew up the list of Cabinet members of which Papen was to be head shows the extent of the army's influence.

... on 26 May 1932 I received a telephone call from General von Schleicher, who asked me to come to Berlin on an urgent matter. I arrived the next day without any idea of what was going on, and on the 28th I called on him at his office. He gave me a general survey of the political situation, described the crisis within the cabinet, and told me that it was the President's wish to form a cabinet of experts, independent of the political parties. It had become technically impossible to form a parliamentary cabinet, because no combination could command a majority. The sole remaining constitutional solution was the formation of a presidential cabinet by the chief of State. Schleicher gave me a colourful description of the impossibility of relying further on Brüning. His unilateral ban on the Brown Shirts had placed the National Socialists even more sharply in opposition, and had at the same time put the President in an embarrassing situation constitutionally *vis-à-vis* the other parties. He no longer considered it possible to combat a party as strong as the Nazis by negative means, which had only resulted in the steady and threatening growth of their power. The Nazis claimed to be actuated by patriotic motives, for which a great many Germans found sympathy, and it was becoming increasingly difficult to prevent the younger Reichswehr officers from being attracted by their ideas.

Brüning had insisted, so Schleicher told me, that he would never sit at the same table with National Socialists. But there was no way of obtaining their cooperation in the affairs of government if they were driven further and further into opposition and exposed to increasingly radical influences. Some solution had to be found. Hindenburg was also perturbed at the manner in which Brüning's emergency financial decrees were depressing the standard of living of those dependent on pensions and investment incomes. The economic crises could only be solved by much more positive methods. The President was no longer convinced that the Chancellor's policies would protect the authority of the State and the country's economy from complete breakdown.

Schleicher left me in no doubt that he was acting as spokesman for the army, the only stable organization remaining in the State, preserved intact and free of party political strife by von Seeckt and his successors. In the present parliamentary crisis, this instrument of law and order could only be spared from intervention in the civil war that threatened, if an authoritarian cabinet were to replace the tottering party system. This was a theme we had often discussed. From my public speeches Schleicher knew of my constant insistence that Brüning should form a national coalition government and return to Bismarck's conception of uniting the post of Chancellor and Prussian Prime Minister, so that the Federal Cabinet might bring the Prussian services of public order under its authority and thus secure the stability of the government.

I therefore found myself in complete agreement with Schleicher's train of thought. . . . He [Schleicher] then turned the conversation to the subject of who could lead the new cabinet. We discussed various names and he asked for my opinion. There had been nothing out of the ordinary in our conversation so far, but to my amazement Schleicher now suggested that I should take over this task myself.

Looking at me with his humorous and somewhat sarcastic smile, he seemed to appreciate my astonishment. 'This offer takes me completely by surprise,' I said. 'I very much doubt if I am the right man. I know we seem to be agreed on the measures that have to be taken, and I shall be glad to help in any way that I can – but Reich Chancellor! That is a very different matter.'

'I have already suggested your name to the Old Gentleman,'

Schleicher said, 'and he is most insistent that you should accept the post.'

Schleicher then took me by the arm and we walked up and down the room, talking of old friends. 'You have simply got to do Hindenburg and myself this service. Everything depends on it, and I cannot think of anyone who would do it better. You are a man of moderate convictions, whom no one will accuse of dictatorial tendencies, and there is no other right-wing man of whom the same could be said. I have even drawn up a provisional cabinet list which I am sure you will approve.'

I had to interrupt him. 'Give me time to think this over, Schleicher,' I said. 'Perhaps I can think of someone better. In any case, we have got to make up our minds what we can offer if we are to get the Nazis to collaborate in a Presidential Cabinet.'

'I have already had a word with Hitler about that,' Schleicher said. 'I told him we would lift the ban on the Brown Shirts, providing they behaved themselves, and dissolve the Reichstag. He has assured me that in return the Nazis would give the cabinet their tacit support, even though they are not represented in it.' . . .

A quarter of an hour later I stood before the President. He received me with his usual paternal kindliness. 'Well, my dear Papen,' he said in his deep voice, 'I hope you are going to help me out of this difficult situation.'

'Herr Reich President, I am afraid I cannot,' I said.

I told him I agreed fully with the necessity for a change of course, and suggested that it might still be possible get Brüning to take the necessary steps. Hindenburg thought there was little chance of this. It was his belief that Brüning had no other solution but that of his emergency decrees. Nor had he been able to convince Brüning that it would not be possible to ban the uniformed formations of the Nazis alone. But his chief complaint was the impossible situation in which he had been placed by his re-election by the left and centre parties alone, while the National Socialists had put up this 'corporal' against him. He had made up his mind to form a Cabinet out of people in whom he had personal confidence and who could govern without having arguments at every step.

I agreed with all this, but tried to convince him with all my powers of persuasion – and Kaas himself could not have been more articulate – that there was no point in calling on me in the hope that I would have the support of the Zentrum Party. If I accepted the post I would only incur the hate and enmity of my own party and he might just as well call upon the German Nationalists for the task.

I have often described the scene that followed. Rising heavily from his chair, the old Field-Marshal put both hands on my shoulders: 'You cannot possibly leave an old man like me in the lurch,' he said. 'In spite of my age I have had to accept the responsibilities of the nation for another period. I am asking you now to take over a task on which the future of our country depends, and I am relying on your sense of duty and patriotism to do what I ask you.' I can remember to this day the deep, heavy tone of his voice, so full of warmth, yet so demanding. 'It is immaterial to me if you earn the disapproval or even the enmity of your party. I intend to have people round me who are independent of political parties, men of good will and expert knowledge, who will surmount the crisis of our country.' The President's voice rose slightly. 'You have been a soldier and did your duty in the war. When the Fatherland calls, Prussia knows only one response – obedience.'

I struck my colours. Such a call, I felt, transcended party obligations. I clasped the Field-Marshal's hand. Schleicher, who had been waiting in the next room, came in to offer his congratulations.

Memoirs. A. Deutsch, London, 1952, pp. 150–3 and 157–8.

14 Darkest Reaction, 1932
COUNT HARRY KESSLER

Berlin. 4 June 1932. Saturday.

Papen's government declaration. A hardly credible document, an extract – written in miserable style – of darkest reaction, compared with which the declarations of the Kaiser's government seem like the brightest Enlightenment. Social insurance is to be reduced, 'cultural Bolshevism' to be combated, the German people to be steeled for the foreign struggle and 'concentrated' on the basis of extreme right-wing Junkerdom by means of a revival of Christianity (for this, read hypocrisy); all other movements and parties – Social Democracy, liberal bourgeoisie, Centre – are attacked as not 'national' and as morally destructive. A government document of such political idiocy and clumsiness, such dark reaction, has not been published since the Polignac government of 1830 [in France]. It clearly bears the stamp of the general staff.

H. Kessler, *Tagebücher 1918–37*, Insel-Verlag, Frankfurt a.M., 1961, p. 670

15 Plans for a Dictatorship
FRANZ VON PAPEN

On 20 July 1932, Papen took over the Prussian government by force and deposed the Social Democratic Prussian Ministers. On 31 July, the Reichstag elections brought the Nazis to their greatest electoral triumph before their 'seizure of power': they gained 230 out of the 608 Reichstag seats. In a further Reichstag election, on 6 November, the Nazis lost two million votes but still held 196 out of 584 seats. Papen and his Cabinet resigned on 17 November 1932. As Hitler still insisted on the Chancellorship, which Hinden-burg refused to concede, Papen tried to persuade Hindenburg to abolish the Reichstag altogether and establish a dictatorship. Schleicher, however, refused to involve the army in a civil war and persuaded Hindenburg to appoint him, Schleicher, Chancellor, with the idea of splitting the Nazis.

... There seemed no reason to suppose that the newly elected Reichstag should not behave in exactly the same way as the previous one. If the government was not going to be permitted to function, then it must do without the Reichstag altogether for a short period. Our proposed amendments to the constitution would then be made the subject of a referendum or submitted for approval to a new National Assembly. This procedure, I realized, would involve a breach of the present constitution by the President.

The situation was so serious that I considered that the President might be justified in placing the welfare of the nation above his oath to the constitution. I told him I realized that this would be a difficult decision for a man who had always placed the value of his word above everything else, but I reminded him of the manner in which Bismarck had once found it necessary to recommend to the Prussian monarch that the constitution should be ignored for the sake of the country. Once the necessary reforms had been voted, it would be possible to return the duties of legislation to the new Parliament.

It was then Schleicher's turn. He said he had a plan which would absolve the President from taking this last drastic step. If he took over the government himself, he thought he could bring about a split in the National Socialist Party which would ensure a parliamentary majority in the present Reichstag. He then gave a detailed explanation of the differences of opinion within the Nazi movement which made it more than likely that he would be able to attract the support of Gregor Strasser and about sixty Nazi members of the Reichstag. Strasser and one or two of his close supporters would be offered posts in the government, which would be based upon the support of the trade unions, the Social Democrats and the bourgeois parties. This would provide a majority which would make it possible to put through the economic and social programme of the Papen government.

Memoirs, pp. 216 f.

16 The Army Supports Hitler as Chancellor, 1933

KURT FREIHERR VON HAMMERSTEIN-EQUORD

Schleicher's failure to split the Nazis had undermined his position by mid-January 1933. On 4 January, Papen had met Hitler in Cologne and promised to press Hindenburg to appoint Hitler as Chancellor. According to the following notes, made by General von Hammerstein in 1935, Schleicher too was now convinced that only Hitler's appointment to the Chancellorship could save the country from civil war.

From about 20 January 1933 onwards, rumours grew that the position of the Reich Chancellor von Schleicher was thoroughly shaken, because Reich President von Hindenburg, acting under the influence of Papen, Hugenberg's backstairs men and Hindenburg's son, wished to withdraw his confidence in him. There was talk of a Papen–Hugenberg cabinet with National Socialist participation. General von Stülpnagel or Herr Schmidt-Hannover were mentioned as possible war ministers, with the rider that the National Socialists might possibly demand and be given the War Ministry.

All this was improbable, as the National Socialists would on no account have entered a Papen–Hugenberg Cabinet. However, the rumours persisted and became stronger still.

On the morning of 26 January I went to see Schleicher and asked him what was true in the rumours about a change in government. Schleicher confirmed that the Reich President would almost certainly withdraw his confidence either today or tomorrow, and that he would resign. I went from Schleicher to State Secretary Meissner, asked him what was to happen after Schleicher's resignation, and told him clearly and unmistakably that the National Socialists would never enter a Papen–Hugenberg cabinet. Such a cabinet would have as enemies the National Socialists on the one hand and the Left from Dingeldey (DVP) to Thälmann (KPD) on the other. It would thus rest on a tiny base. The army would then have to support this 7 per cent base against 93 per cent of the German people. That would be dangerous to the highest degree; could such a solution be avoided?

Meissner evidently judged the situation similarly and arranged for me to report my concern to the Reich President immediately. This I did. Hindenburg angrily forbade me to intervene in political matters, but then said, apparently to reassure me, 'that he had no intention of making the Austrian lance-corporal War Minister or Reich Chancellor. . . .'

Hindenburg failed to understand my fear that the army might become involved or be misused in a fight between Papen–Hugenberg on the one hand and the National Socialists and the entire Left on the other. I departed with my fears increased, for Schleicher's dismissal was already settled. What was to follow was obviously completely unclear.

On 29 January a discussion took place in my office between . . . Schleicher and myself. We were both convinced that only Hitler was possible as future Reich Chancellor. Any other choice would lead to a general strike, if not to civil war, and thus to a totally undesirable use of the army against the National Socialists as well as against the Left. We considered whether we knew of any other way to influence the situation to avoid this misfortune. The result of our considerations was negative. We saw no possibility of exercising any further influence on the Reich President. Finally I decided, in agreement with Schleicher, to seek a meeting with Hitler.

K. D. Bracher, *Die Auflösung der Weimarer Republik.* Villingen, 1955, pp. 733 f.

17 Political Testament, 1934
PAUL VON HINDENBURG

Hindenburg wrote his Political Testament on 11 May 1934, shortly before his death. The authenticity of this document was questioned when published by Hitler, but it is now clear that the Nazis had no need to tamper with it. It is true, however, that Hindenburg also expressed the wish, in a private letter to Hitler, that the monarchy be restored, and that Hitler did not publish this letter.

To the German nation and its Chancellor, my testament.
In 1919 I wrote in my message to the German nation: 'We were at the end! Like Siegfried under the cunning javelin of the furious Hagen, our exhausted front collapsed. In vain had we endeavoured to drink new life from the perennial spring of native strength. It was our task now to save the remaining strength of our army for the later reconstruction of the Fatherland. The present was lost. There remained now only hope – and the future!

'I understand the idea of escape from the world which obsessed many officers, in view of the collapse of all that was dear and true to them. The desire to know nothing more of a world where seething passions obscured the vital qualities of our nation so that they could no longer be recognized, is humanly conceivable. And yet – but I must express it frankly, just as I think! Comrades of the once grand, proud German army! Can you speak of losing heart? Think of the men who more than a hundred years ago created for us a new Fatherland. Their religion was their faith in themselves and in the sanctity of their cause. They created the new Fatherland, basing it not on freak doctrinaire theories foreign to our nature, but building it up on the foundations of the free development of the framework and the principles of our own common weal! When it is able, Germany will go along this way again.

'I have the firm conviction that now, as in those times, the links with our great rich past will be preserved, and, where they have been broken, will be restored. The old German spirit will again assert itself triumphantly, though only after thorough purgings in the fires of suffering and passion.

'Our opponents knew the strength of this spirit; they admired and hated it in times of peace; they were astonished at it and feared it on the battlefields of the Great War. They sought to explain our strength to their peoples by using the empty word "organization". They passed over in silence the spirit which lived and moved behind the veil of this word. But in and with this spirit we will again courageously construct.

'Germany, the focus-point of so many of the inexhaustible values of human civilization and culture, will not go under so long as it retains faith in its historical world mission. I have the sure confidence that the depth and strength of thought of the best in our Fatherland will succeed in blending new ideas with the precious treasures of former times, and from them will forge in concert lasting values for the welfare of our Fatherland.

'This is the unshakable conviction with which I leave the bloody battlefield of international warfare. I have seen the heroic agony of my Fatherland and never, never will believe that it was its death agony.

'For the present our entire former constitution lies buried under the flood-tide raised by the storm of wild political passions and resounding phrases which has apparently destroyed all sacred traditions. But this flood-tide will subside. Then, from the eternally agitated sea of human life, will again emerge that rock to which the hope of our fathers clung, that rock upon which, nearly half a century ago, the future of our Fatherland was, by our strength, confidently founded – the German Empire! When the national idea, the national consciousness, has again been raised, then, out of the Great War – on which no nation can look back with such legitimate pride and with such clear conscience as we – as well as out of the bitter severity of the present days, precious moral fruits will ripen for us. The blood of all those who have fallen in the faith of the greatness of the Fatherland will not then have flowed in vain. In this assurance I lay down my pen and rely firmly on you – the Youth of Germany.'

I wrote these words in the darkest hours and in the conviction that

I was fast approaching the close of a life spent in the service of the Fatherland. Fate disposed otherwise for me. In the spring of 1925 a new chapter of my life was opened. Again I was wanted to cooperate in the destiny of my nation. Only my firm confidence in Germany's inexhaustible resources gave me the courage to accept the office of *Reichspräsident*. This firm belief lent me also the moral strength to fulfil unswervingly the duties of that difficult position.

The last chapter of my life has been for me, at the same time, the most difficult. Many have not understood me in these troublous times and have not comprehended that my only anxiety was to lead the distracted and discouraged German nation back to self-conscious unity.

I began and conducted the duties of my office in the consciousness that a preparatory period of complete renunciation was necessary in domestic and international politics. From the Easter message of the year 1925 – in which I exhorted the nation to the fear of God, to social justice, to internal peace and political sanity – onwards, I have become tired of cultivating the inward unity of our nation and the self-consciousness of its best qualities. Moreover, I was conscious that the political constitution and form of government which were provided for the nation in the hour of its greatest distress and greatest weakness did not correspond with the requirements and characteristics of our people. The time must arrive when this knowledge would become general. It therefore seemed my duty to rescue the country from the morass of external oppression and degradation, internal distress and self-disruption, without jeopardizing its existence, before this hour struck.

The guardian of the State, the Reichswehr, must be the symbol and firm support for this superstructure. On the Reichswehr, as a firm foundation, must rest the old Prussian virtues of self-realized dutifulness, of simplicity, and comradeship. The German Reichswehr had, after the collapse, cultivated the continuation of the high traditions of the old army in typical style. Always and at all times the Reichswehr must remain the pattern of State conduct, so that, unbiased by any internal political development, its lofty mission for the defence of the country may be put to good account.

When I shall have returned to my comrades above, with whom I have fought on so many battlefields for the honour and glory of the nation, then I shall call to the younger generation:

'Show yourselves worthy of your ancestors, and never forget, if you would secure the peace and well-being of your native country, that you must be prepared to give up everything for its peace and honour. Never forget that your deeds will one day become tradition.'

The thanks of the Field-Marshal of the World War and its Commander-in-Chief are due to all the men who have accomplished the construction and organization of the Reichswehr.

Internationally the German nation had to wander through a Gethsemane. A frightful treaty weighed heavily upon it, and through its increasingly evil effects threatened to bring about the collapse of our nation. For a long time the surrounding world did not understand that Germany must live, not only for its own sake, but also for the sake of Europe and as the standard-bearer of western culture. Only step by step, without awaking an overwhelming resistance, were the fetters which bound us to be loosened. If many of my comrades at that time did not understand the difficulties that beset our path, history will certainly judge rightly, how severe, but also how necessary in the interests of the maintenance of German existence, was many a State act signed by me.

In unison with the growing internal recovery and strengthening of the German nation, a progressive and – God willing – a generous contribution towards the solution of all troublesome European questions could be striven after and obtained, on the basis of its own national honour and dignity. I am thankful to Providence that, in the evening of my life, I have been allowed to see this hour of the nation's renewal of strength. I thank all those who, by unselfish devotion to the Fatherland, have cooperated with me in the reconstruction of Germany. My Chancellor, Adolf Hitler, and his movement have together led the German nation above all professional and class distinctions, to internal unity – a decided step of historical importance. I know that much remains to be done, and I desire with my whole heart that the act of reconciliation which embraces the entire German Fatherland may be the forerunner of the act of national exaltation and national cooperation.

I depart from my German people in the full hope that what I longed for in the year 1919, and which was coming slowly to fruition in January 1933, may mature to the complete fulfilment and perfection of the historical mission of our nation.

In this firm belief in the future of the Fatherland, I close my eyes in peace.

J. W. Wheeler-Bennett, *Hindenburg, The Wooden Titan*. New York, 1967, pp. 470–3.

VII
Hitler's Foreign Aims

The most frightening aspects of Hitler's foreign programme were its simplicity and its consistency. 'I have the gift of reducing all problems to their simplest form', said Hitler. All the evidence now available, from the earliest speeches, through his *Mein Kampf* (1924), his *Second Book* (1928), his conversations with Rauschning (1932-4), his meetings with foreign statesmen and diplomats in 1939-41, to his *Table Talk* and *War Directives* of the war years, points in the same direction. His aims were: to seize power; to exploit the Allies' bad conscience about Versailles; to conquer the whole of Europe; to turn the east, up to the Urals and the Caspian Sea, into a slave colony; to establish a colonial empire in Africa; and to prepare for the final struggle (which he thought would take place after his death) for world domination against England and America. In geographical extent, his European aims were very similar to those pursued by Imperial Germany towards the end of the First World War. His eastern aims differed in *quality* very considerably from the aims of Ludendorff, however. The Russians and the Poles were to live, as Professor Trevor-Roper has written, 'as a depressed Helot class, hewing wood and drawing water for a privileged aristocracy of German colonists who will sit in fortified cities, connected by strategic autobahns, glorifying in their nationality and listening to *The Merry Widow* for ever and ever'. Intimately linked to this programme was his plan to liquidate the Jews, for he considered that they were the real power behind Bolshevik Russia. In pursuing the early stages of this programme, Hitler had the support not only of the German 'establishment' but of large sections of the German people as well, for few had accepted the reality of military defeat in 1918. For the execution of his eastern aims, however, Hitler had to rely more and more on the S.S. alone, and to keep the truth from the German people as much as possible.

1 A Comparison of German Aims in the Two World Wars

FRITZ FISCHER

The following passage, which points out the similarities – but also the differ-ences – between the official German war aims in the two world wars, is taken from a lecture on 'Continuity in Recent German History' delivered by Professor Fischer at Sussex University in the spring of 1968. It is printed here with the kind permission of the author.

From the personal point of view there are, without doubt, deep differ-ences between such men as Bethmann Hollweg and Kühlmann or also the Kaiser and Ludendorff on the one hand, and Hitler and his followers on the other. However, the similarity in the directions, even if not in the essence of German aims in the two world wars is striking. This similarity can be traced to the geographic position of Germany as well as to the continuity of ideas about the position of Germany in Europe and the world.

If we look at German war aims in the west, we find in the First as in the Second World War the desire to weaken France and to incor-porate her into a political or economic system under German domin-ance. The re-annexation of Alsace-Lorraine in the Second World War was a matter of course, as was its enlargement – already aimed at in the First World War – by the iron ore region of Longwy-Briey. In such a system, dominated by Germany, at least economically, Luxemburg, Belgium and Holland were also to be incorporated, as were the Scandinavian States.

Looking to the east, in both wars Poland was to be a satellite state, diminished by a 'border-strip', whose size in the First World War was a matter of dispute between the military and the more moderate government. In the Second World War the size of this 'border-strip' – after the re-annexation of the 'Corridor' and Posen and Upper Silesia – was as big (it included Lodz) as only the Pan-Germans had dreamed of in the First World War. By further direct annexations the rest of Poland in the First World War as in the Second World War was to be separated from Lithuania and the Baltic States. In both wars the intention was to annex the Baltic States directly to the Reich, so as to 'save' the Baltic Germans, a hopelessly small minority in these territories. Finland (from 1808 a Russian territory, although with some autonomy) was to be revolutionized in the First World War, and an expeditionary force helped to separate it from the new Bolshevik Russia; in the Second World War it was won as an ally against Soviet Russia. The weakening of Russia, already begun by the separation of Poland, the Baltic States and Finland, was to be achieved decisively by the separation of the Ukraine. By supplying raw materials to Germany and by buying goods the Ukraine (as a sort of satellite State) was to become a basis for the German world power position, as were the Crimea and the Caucasus with Georgia, with their rich mineral oil and manganese resources.

However, in looking at the eastern territories as a whole, a profound difference should not be overlooked: whereas in the First World War German policies in the Ukraine (as well as in Finland, Poland, Georgia, etc.) supported a movement for autonomy or even separation from Russia, in the Second World War Hitler's chief ideologist, Alfred Rosenberg, who maintained similar ideas of 'liberating' the Ukraine and all non-Russian nationalities from the Soviet rule, failed to prevail over the ideas of Hitler and Himmler, who wished to treat the peoples of the east (including the Poles) solely as serfs under a German master race. Not until very late, too late for his Reich, did Hitler return to the liberation ideology of Rosenberg by building up the Vlassov army. This idea to treat millions of Russians as serfs, as helots, a mixture of romanticism and brutality, did not exist in the First World War. In 1917-8 a Russia freed from the Bolsheviks or Bolshevik Russia itself (which had signed the Treaty of Brest-Litovsk) was regarded as a sort of ally in the continuing struggle with the western powers.

If we look towards the south-east, in the First World War Turkey was an ally of Germany, destined to fall into economic and political dependence on Germany; in the Second World War the same aim was pursued by the mission of von Papen, but was blocked by the counter-measures taken by England. An attempt was made in both wars to bring revolution to North Africa, to Egypt, Syria and Iraq. The most important aim, however, was the incorporation of the Balkans into the German system, especially Rumania in view of her resources of mineral oil. In the First World War this was achieved by the conquest of the territory (after Rumania had entered the war on the side of the Allies) and the Treaty of Bucharest; in the Second World War by the occupation of the country and its position as a satellite-ally. In a similar way Serbia/Yugoslavia was conquered in the First World War and in the Second World War, in the latter case becoming a region of partisan warfare.

The connecting link between the direct or indirect enlargement of Germany in the east and in the west had been in the First World War the idea of *Mitteleuropa* (central Europe), which was supported by many German economists and was suggested to Bethmann Hollweg by Walther Rathenau. At the beginning the inclusion of France, Belgium and Poland was the primary aim; after the battle of the Marne all effort was concentrated on the political, military and economic union with Austria-Hungary.

The *Anschluss* of Austria and the annexation of the Sudetenland before the Second World War was a step in the same direction. The *Anschluss* was, however, in no way Hitler's invention, but had its origin in the unanimous decision of the Austrian National Assembly in 1918 (after the downfall of the monarchy and the break-up of the multinational empire) to join the new German Republic (a similar demand was made by the Sudeten-Germans through their representative bodies). The treaties of St. Germain and Versailles, which prevented the realization of this desire and this decision, were passionately resented as a violation of the proclaimed principle of self-determination. In the Weimar Republic the Social Democrats and the Catholics, especially in southern Germany, were the main supporters of the idea of *Anschluss*, whereas the Protestant north-east concentrated its interest on the regaining of the 'Corridor', lost to the new Poland. During the negotiations (frustrated by France) for a customs union between Austria and Germany, conducted by the Austrian Chancellor Schober and Reich Chancellor Brüning, the idea was discussed that such a customs and economic union would by its very nature draw Czechoslovakia into this greater unit. The union would thus have established a connection which Hitler later established in a brutal form by breaking the recently concluded treaty of Munich and occupying Czechoslovakia in March 1939.

Finally it should not be forgotten that before and during the First World War the aim of a coherent *Mittelafrika* was pursued. A map of the German Admiralty drawn up during the Second World War shows that the same aim was kept after 1933. Hitler himself, however, had directed all his interest on the *Ostraum* (the eastern regions) because – subjectively perhaps sincere in his love-hate relationship towards the English 'master race' – he was ready to let England have its overseas Empire or even to 'guarantee' it to her in exchange for an alliance.

Much as the aims may have differed in detail and in the means used to achieve them, one thing one cannot deny: the aim was, and the effect would have been, had Germany been victorious, the domination of the German Empire on the European continent, a German hegemony, achieved either against England or with its consent. Only of secondary importance is the question whether this aim is to be regarded as defensive – as the breaking up of the 'encirclement' of Germany by the Triple Entente, which subjectively was felt as menacing – or whether this aim was aggressive – expansionist, influenced by the master race ideology. In order to prevent this domination of Europe by one power, not only did England and Russia resist to the utmost, but twice America had to enter the war, as a result of which the position of Europe itself was altered fundamentally.

2 The Hossbach Memorandum, 1937

On 5 November 1937, Hitler called a conference at the Reich Chancellery. Present were General von Blomberg, the Minister of War, von Neurath, the Foreign Minister, and Fritsch, Raeder and Goering, commanders of the army, navy and air force respectively. Colonel von Hossbach drafted this protocol of the meeting several days afterwards, whether on the basis of notes or from memory is still disputed.

The Führer began by stating that the subject of the present conference was of such importance that its discussion would, in other countries, certainly be a matter for a full cabinet meeting, but he – the Führer – had rejected the idea of making it a subject of discussion before the wider circle of the Reich cabinet just because of the importance of the matter. His exposition to follow was the fruit of thorough deliberation and the experiences of his four-and-a-half years of power. He wished to explain to the gentlemen present his basic ideas concerning the opportunities for the development of our position in the field of foreign affairs and its requirements, and he asked, in the interests of a long-term German policy, that his exposition be regarded, in the event of his death, as his last will and testament.

149

The Führer then continued:

The aim of German policy was to make secure and to preserve the racial community [*Volksmasse*] and to enlarge it. It was therefore a question of space. . . .

Germany's problem could only be solved by means of force and this was never without attendant risk. The campaigns of Frederick the Great for Silesia and Bismarck's wars against Austria and France had involved unheard-of risk, and the swiftness of the Prussian action in 1870 had kept Austria from entering the war. If one accepts as the basis of the following exposition the resort to force with its attendant risks, then there remain still to be answered the questions 'when' and 'how'. In this matter there were three cases [*Fälle*] to be dealt with:

Case 1:   Period 1943–5.
After this date only a change for the worse, from our point of view, could be expected.

The equipment of the army, navy, and *Luftwaffe*, as well as the formation of the officer corps, was nearly completed. Equipment and armament were modern; in further delay there lay the danger of their obsolescence. In particular, the secrecy of 'special weapons' could not be preserved forever. The recruiting of reserves was limited to current age groups; further drafts from older untrained age groups were no longer available.

Our relative strength would decrease in relation to the rearmament which would by then have been carried out by the rest of the world. If we did not act by 1943–5, any year could, in consquence of a lack of reserves, produce the food crisis, to cope with which the necessary foreign exchange was not available, and this must be regarded as a 'warning of the régime'. Besides, the world was expecting our attack and was increasing its counter-measures from year to year. It was while the rest of the world was still preparing its defences [*sich abriegele*] that we were obliged to take the offensive.

Nobody knew today what the situation would be in the years 1943–5. One thing only was certain, that we could not wait longer.

On the one hand there was the great *Wehrmacht*, and the necessity of maintaining it at its present level, the ageing of the movement and of its leaders; and on the other, the prospect of a lowering of the standard of living and of a limitation of the birth rate, which left no choice but to act. If the Führer was still living, it was his unalterable resolve to solve Germany's problem of space at the latest by 1943–5.

The necessity for action before 1943–5 would arise in cases 2 and 3.

Case 2:

If internal strife in France should develop into such a domestic crisis as to absorb the French army completely and render it incapable of use for war against Germany, then the time for action against the Czechs had come.

Case 3:

If France is so embroiled by a war with another State that she cannot 'proceed' against Germany. . . .

On the assumption of a development of the situation leading to action on our part as planned, in the years 1943–5, the attitude of France, Britain, Italy, Poland and Russia could probably be estimated as follows:

Actually, the Führer believed that almost certainly Britain, and probably France as well, had already tacitly written off the Czechs and were reconciled to the fact that this question would be cleared up in due course by Germany. Difficulties connected with the Empire, and the prospect of being once more entangled in a protracted European war, were decisive considerations for Britain against participation in a war against Germany. Britain's attitude would certainly not be without influence on that of France. An attack by France without British support, and with the prospect of the offensive being brought to a standstill on our western fortifications, was hardly probable. Nor was a French march through Belgium and Holland without British support to be expected; this also was a course not to be contemplated by us in the event of a conflict with France, because it would certainly entail the hostility of Britain. It would of course be necessary to maintain a strong defence [*eine Abriegelung*] on our western frontier during the prosecution of our attack on the Czechs and Austria. And in this connection it had to be remembered that the defence measures of the Czechs were growing in strength from year to year, and that the actual worth of the Austrian army also was increasing in the course of time. Even though the populations concerned, especially Czechoslovakia, were not sparse, the annexation of Czechoslovakia and Austria would mean an acquisition of foodstuff for 5 to 6 million people, on the assumption that the compulsory emigration of 2 million people from Czechoslovakia and 1 million people from Austria was practicable. The incorporation of these two States with Germany meant, from the politico-military point of view, a substantial advantage because it would mean shorter and better frontiers, the freeing of forces for other purposes, and the possibility of creating new units up to a level of about 12 divisions, that is, 1 new division per million inhabitants.

Italy was not expected to object to the elimination of the Czechs, but it was impossible at the moment to estimate what her attitude on the Austrian question would be; that depended essentially upon whether the Duce were still alive.

The degree of surprise and the swiftness of our action were decisive factors for Poland's attitude. Poland – with Russia at her rear – will have little inclination to engage in war against a victorious Germany.

Military intervention by Russia must be countered by the swiftness of our operations; however, whether such an intervention was a practical contingency at all was, in view of Japan's attitude, more than doubtful.

Should case 2 arise – the crippling of France by civil war–the situation thus created by the elimination of the most dangerous opponents must be seized upon *whenever it occurs* for the blow against the Czechs.

The Führer saw case 3 coming definitely nearer; it might emerge from the present tensions in the Mediterranean, and he was resolved to take advantage of it whenever it happened, even as early as 1938.

Documents of German Foreign Policy, 1918–1945. Series D, Volume I. London, H.M.S.O., 1949, pp. 29 ff.

3 The Obersalzberg Speech, 1939

ADOLF HITLER

On 22 August 1939, Hitler addressed the commanding generals of his army. No less than six records of the speech have now been discovered, and all of them basically agree. This version was handed to the British ambassador by an American journalist on 25 August, after the American ambassador had refused to accept it as being too dangerous. It now seems likely that the report was given to the journalist by someone close to Admiral Canaris, who attended the conference and became one of the key figures in the conspiracy against Hitler.

Decision to attack Poland was arrived at in spring. Originally there was fear that because of the political constellation we would have to strike at the same time against England, France, Russia and Poland. This risk too we should have had to take. Goering had demonstrated to us that his Four-Year Plan is a failure and that we are at the end of our strength, if we do not achieve victory in a coming war.

Since the autumn of 1938 and since I have realized that Japan will not go with us unconditionally and that Mussolini is endangered by that nitwit of a King and the treacherous scoundrel of a Crown Prince, I decided to go with Stalin. After all there are only three great statesmen in the world, Stalin, I and Mussolini. Mussolini is the weakest, for he has been able to break the power neither of the crown nor of the Church. Stalin and I are the only ones who visualize the future. So in a few weeks hence I shall stretch out my hand to Stalin at the common German–Russian frontier and with him undertake to redistribute the world.

Our strength lies in our quickness and in our brutality; Genghis Khan has sent millions of women and children into death knowingly and with a light heart. History sees in him only the great founder of States. As to what the weak western European civilization asserts about me, that is of no account. I have given the command and I shall shoot everyone who utters one word of criticism, for the goal to be obtained in the war is not that of reaching certain lines but of physically demolishing the opponent. And so for the present only in the east I have put my death-head formation in place with the command relentlessly and without compassion to send into death many women and children of Polish origin and language. Only thus we can gain the living space that we need. Who after all is today speaking about the destruction of the Armenians?

Colonel-General von Brauchitsch has promised me to bring the war against Poland to a close within a few weeks. Had he reported to me that he needs two years or even only one year, I should not have given the command to march and should have allied myself temporarily with England instead of Russia for we cannot conduct a long war. To be sure a new situation has arisen. I experienced those poor worms Daladier and Chamberlain in Munich. They will be too cowardly to attack. They won't go beyond a blockade. Against that we have our autarchy and the Russian raw materials.

Poland will be depopulated and settled with Germans. My pact with the Poles was merely conceived of as a gaining of time. As for the rest, gentlemen, the fate of Russia will be exactly the same as I am now going through with in the case of Poland. After Stalin's death – he is a very sick man – we will break the Soviet Union. Then there will begin the dawn of the German rule of the earth.

The little States cannot scare me. After Kemal's death Turkey is governed by '*cretins*' and half idiots. Carol of Rumania is through and through the corrupt slave of his sexual instincts. The King of Belgium and the Nordic kings are soft jumping jacks who are dependent upon the good digestions of their over-eating and tired peoples.

We shall have to take into the bargain the defection of Japan. I gave Japan a full year's time. The Emperor is a counterpart to the last Tsar – weak, cowardly, undecided. May he become a victim of the revolution. My going together with Japan never was popular. We shall continue to create disturbances in the Far East and in Arabia. Let us think as 'gentlemen' and let us see in these peoples at best lacquered half maniacs who are anxious to experience the whip.

The opportunity is as favourable as never before. I have but one worry, namely that Chamberlain or some other such pig of a fellow ('Saukerl') will come at the last moment with proposals or with ratting ('Umfall'). He will fly down the stairs, even if I shall personally have to trample on his belly in the eyes of the photographers.

No, it is too late for this. The attack upon and the destruction of Poland begins Saturday, [26 August,] early. I shall let a few companies in Polish uniform attack in Upper Silesia or in the Protectorate. Whether the world believes it is quite indifferent ('Scheissegal'). The world believes only in success.

For you, gentlemen, fame and honour are beginning as they have not since centuries. Be hard, be without mercy, act more quickly and brutally than the others. The citizens of western Europe must tremble with horror. That is the most humane way of conducting a war. For it scares the others off.

The new method of conducting war corresponds to the new drawing of the frontiers. A war extending from Reval, Lublin, Kaschau to the mouth of the Danube. The rest will be given to the Russians. Ribbentrop has orders to make every offer and to accept every demand. In the west I reserve to myself the right to determine the strategically best line. Here one will be able to work with Protectorate regions, such as Holland, Belgium and French Lorraine.

And now, on to the enemy, in Warsaw we will celebrate our reunion.

The speech was received with enthusiasm. Goering jumped on a table, thanked bloodthirstily and made bloodthirsty promises. He danced like a wild man. The few that had misgivings remained quiet.

Documents of British Foreign Policy. Third Series, Vol. 7, H.M.S.O. pp. 258–9

4 Continental Hegemony, 1941

ADOLF HITLER

26–7 October 1941

For me, the object is to exploit the advantage of continental hegemony. It is ridiculous to think of a world policy as long as one does not control the Continent. The Spaniards, the Dutch, the French and ourselves have learnt that by experience. When we are masters of Europe, we have a dominant position in the world. A hundred and thirty million people in the Reich, ninety in the Ukraine. Add to these the other States of the New Europe, and we'll be four hundred millions, compared with the hundred and thirty million Americans.

If the British Empire collapsed today, it would be thanks to our arms, but we'd get no benefit, for we wouldn't be the heirs. Russia would take India, Japan would take Eastern Asia, the United States would take Canada. I couldn't even prevent the Americans from gaining a firm hold in Africa.

H. R. Trevor-Roper (ed.), *Hitler's Table Talk*, Weidenfeld and Nicolson, 1953, p. 93.

5 Burgundy, Wallonia, Northern France, 1942

ADOLF HITLER

Hitler's aims in the West were more extensive than those defined by Bethmann Hollweg in 1914, but not much more so than those demanded by certain other leading figures during the First World War.

25 April 1942

For my part, I see in the escape of this general [de Gaulle] . . . a significant pointer to the real attitude of the French towards us. We must therefore keep a very cool head in our dealings with them, both now during the armistice period and later when the peace treaty is formulated; and we must bear in mind all historical precedents and take decisions in which sentiment plays no part. We must not be content with the control of the Atlantic (i.e. Channel) Islands. If we are to ensure the hegemony of the Continent, we must also retain strong-points on what was formerly the Atlantic coast. We must further not forget that the old Kingdom of Burgundy played a prominent rôle in German history and that it is from time immemorial German soil, which the French grabbed at the time of our weakness. . . .

5 May 1942

. . . This work, published in 1937, further strengthens my conviction that Wallonia and northern France are in reality German lands. The abundance of German-sounding place-names, the widespread customs of Germanic origin, the forms of idiom which have persisted – all these prove, to my mind, that these territories have been systematically detached, not to say snatched, from the Germanic territories.

If there are territories anywhere which we have every right to reclaim, then it is these.

H. R. Trevor-Roper (ed.), *Hitler's Table Talk*, pp. 442 and 460.

6 The German New Order in the East, 1941-2

ADOLF HITLER

27 July 1941

We must take care to prevent a military power from ever again establishing itself on this side of the Urals, for our neighbours to the west would always be allied with our neighbours to the east. That's how the French once made common cause with the Turks, and now the English are behaving in the same fashion with the Soviets. When I say, on this side of the Urals, I mean a line running two or three hundred kilometres east of the Urals.

It should be possible for us to control this region to the east with two hundred and fifty thousand men plus a cadre of good administrators. Let's learn from the English, who, with two hundred and fifty thousand men in all, including fifty thousands soldiers, govern four hundred million Indians. This space in Russia must always be dominated by Germans.

Nothing would be a worse mistake on our part than to seek to educate the masses there. It is in our interest that the people should know just enough to recognize the signs on the roads. At present they can't read and they ought to stay like that. But they must be allowed to live decently, of course, and that's also to our interest.

We'll take the southern part of the Ukraine, especially the Crimea, and make it an exclusively German colony. There'll be no harm in pushing out the population that's there now. The German colonist will be the soldier-peasant, and for that I'll take professional soldiers, whatever their line may have been previously. In this way we shall dispose, moreover, of a body of courageous N.C.O.s, whenever we need them. In future we shall have a standing army of a million and a half to two million men. With the discharge of soldiers after twelve years of service, we shall have thirty to forty thousand men to do what we like with every year. For those of them who are sons of peasants, the Reich will put at their disposal a completely equipped farm. The soil costs us nothing, we have only the house to build. The peasant's son will already have paid for it by his twelve years' service. During the last two years he will already be equipping himself for agriculture.

157

One single condition will be imposed upon him: that he may not marry a townswoman, but a countrywoman who, as far as possible, will not have begun to live in a town with him. These soldier-peasants will be given arms, so that at the slightest danger they can be at their posts when we summon them. . . .

8–11 August 1941

The German colonist [in the east] ought to live on handsome, spacious farms. The German services will be lodged in marvellous buildings, the governors in palaces. Beneath the shelter of the administrative services, we shall gradually organize all that is indispensable to the maintenance of a certain standard of living. Around the city, to a depth of thirty to forty kilometres, we shall have a belt of handsome villages connected by the best roads. What exists beyond that will be another world, in which we mean to let the Russians live as they like. It is merely necessary that we should rule them. In the event of a revolution, we shall only have to drop a few bombs on their cities, and the affair will be liquidated. Once a year we shall lead a troop of Kirghizes through the capital of the Reich, in order to strike their imaginations with the size of our monuments. . . .

17–18 September 1941

The Germanic race created the notion of the State. It incarnated this notion in reality, by compelling the individual to be a part of a whole. It's our duty continually to arouse the forces that slumber in our people's blood.

The Slav peoples are not destined to live a cleanly life. They know it, and we would be wrong to persuade them of the contrary. It was we who, in 1918, created the Baltic countries and the Ukraine. But nowadays we have no interest in maintaining Baltic States, any more than in creating an independent Ukraine. We must likewise prevent them from returning to Christianity. That would be a grave fault, for it would be giving them a form of organization.

I'm not a partisan, either, of a university at Kiev. It's better not to teach them to read. They won't love us for tormenting them with schools. Even to give them a locomotive to drive would be a mistake. And what stupidity it would be on our part to proceed with the distribution of land! In spite of that, we'll see to it that the natives live better than they've lived hitherto. We'll find among them the human material that's indispensable for tilling the soil. . . .

We'll supply the Ukrainians with scarves, glass beads and everything that colonial peoples like.

The Germans – this is essential – will have to constitute among themselves a closed society, like a fortress. The least of our stable-lads must be superior to any native.

For German youth, this will be a magnificent field of experiments. We'll attract to the Ukraine Danes, Dutch, Norwegians, Swedes. The army will find areas for manoeuvres there, and our aviation will have the space it needs.

Let's avoid repeating the mistakes committed in the colonies before 1914. Apart from the *Kolonialgesellschaft*, which represented the interests of the State, only the silver interest had any chance of raising their heads there.

The Germans must acquire the feeling for the great, open spaces. We must arrange things so that every German can realize for himself what they mean. We'll take them on trips to the Crimea and the Caucasus. There's a big difference between seeing these countries on the map and actually having visited them.

The railways will serve for the transport of goods, but the roads are what will open the country for us.

Today everybody is dreaming of a world peace conference. For my part, I prefer to wage war for another ten years rather than be cheated thus of the spoils of victory. In any case, my demands are not exorbitant. I'm only interested, when all is said, in territories where Germans have lived before.

The German people will raise itself to the level of this empire. . . .

2 July 1942

I have just read a report by Gauleiter Frauenfeld on the South Tyrol. In it he proposes that the South Tyrolese should be transplanted *en masse* to the Crimea, and I think the idea is an excellent one. There are few places on earth in which a race can better suceed in maintaining its integrity for centuries on end than the Crimea. . . . Their transfer to the Crimea presents neither physical nor psychological difficulty. All they have to do is to sail down just one German waterway, the Danube, and there they are.

H. R. Trevor-Roper (ed.), *Hitler's Table Talk*, pp. 15–16, 24, 34–5, 548.

7 A Page of Glory in Our History, 1943

HEINRICH HIMMLER

In 1942, Hitler complained that he would have achieved nothing but for the S.S. Himmler's speech to S.S. officers in Posen of October 1943 epitomizes the mentality of these, the most dedicated Nazis.

We must be honest, decent, loyal and comradely to members of our own blood, but to nobody else. What happens to a Russian or to a Czech does not interest me in the slightest. What the nations can offer in the way of good blood of our type, we will take, if necessary by kidnapping their children and raising them here with us. Whether nations live in prosperity or starve to death interests me only in so far as we need them for slaves for our *Kultur;* otherwise, it is of no interest to me. Whether 10,000 Russian females fall down from exhaustion digging an anti-tank ditch interests me only in so far as the anti-tank ditch for Germany is finished. . . . It is a crime against our blood to worry about them and give them ideals, thus causing our sons and grandsons to have a more difficult time with them. When somebody comes to me and says, 'I cannot dig the anti-tank ditch with women and children, it is inhuman because it will kill them', then I must reply, 'You are a murderer of our own blood, because if the anti-tank ditch is not dug, German soldiers will die, and they are the sons of German mothers. They are our own blood.' That is what to instill into the S.S. and what I believe I have instilled into them as one of the most sacred laws of the future. . . . I want the S.S. to adopt this attitude to the problem of all foreign, non-Germanic peoples, especially Russians. . . .

Among ourselves it should be mentioned quite frankly – but we will never speak of it publicly. . . . I mean cleaning out the Jews, the extermination of the Jewish race. It is one of those things it's easy to talk about. – 'The Jewish race is being exterminated . . . it's our programme, and we're doing it'. And then they come, eighty million worthy Germans, and each one of them has his worthy Jew. Of course the others are vermin, but this particular Jew is a first-rate man. . . . Most of *you* must know what it means when a hundred corpses are lying side by side, or five hundred or five thousand. To have stuck it out and at the same time (apart from exceptions caused by human weakness) to have remained decent fellows, that is what has made us so hard. This is a page of glory in our history which has never been written and will never be written.

Manvell and Fraenkel, *Heinrich Himmler*. Heinemann, 1965, pp. 135–6.

8 Hitler Orders the Liquidation of the Polish Intelligentsia, 1940

HANS FRANK

Hans Frank was Governor-General of Poland. On 30 May 1940 he explained to his colleagues that he had orders from Hitler to murder potential resistance leaders in Poland.

If thousands of the best Germans must now be sacrificed every minute and every second in the west, then we National Socialists have the duty to ensure that the Polish nation does not rise at the expense of these German sacrifices. That is why I chose this moment to discuss . . . this exceptional pacification programme, which had the aim of ridding the world of the mass of rebellious resistance politicians and other politically suspect individuals who are in our hands. . . . I admit quite openly that this will cost several thousand Poles their life, especially as far as the intellectual leadership class of Poland is concerned. For us all, as National Socialists, the times impose the duty to ensure that the Polish people will never again be capable of resistance. I know what responsiblity we are thereby assuming. . . . I ask you, gentlemen, to help us in the execution of this duty with all the strength at your command. . . . I appeal to you as National Socialist fighters, and I need surely say no more. We shall carry out these measures, and – this I can tell you in confidence – we shall do so in accordance with a command issued to me by the Führer . . .

Gentlemen, we are not murderers. For the policeman and the S.S. man who is compelled, by reason of his office, to carry out these executions, this is a terrible task. We can easily sign hundreds of death warrants; but to ask German men, respectable German soldiers and comrades, to carry out these sentences, that means imposing a terrible burden. . . . Every police officer and S.S. leader who has the hard duty of carrying out these death sentences must be one hundred per cent certain that he is merely carrying out a legal sentence passed by the German Nation. Therefore the summary court procedure must also be applied in these cases . . . so that there is no possibility of the impression arising that this is an arbitrary act.

Buchheim *et al.*, *Die Anatomie des SS-Staates*, Vol. I, pp. 271–3.

9 The Wannsee Conference, 1942

Before 1939, German and later Austrian Jews were persecuted and deprived of their civil rights, but, provided that they were willing to leave their possessions behind and had somewhere to go, they were free to emigrate. With the outbreak of war emigration became impossible. The killing of Polish Jews began soon after the opening of the military campaign, and shortly afterwards, the first deportations of Jews from the rest of German-controlled Europe to Poland began. All were imprisoned in ghettos surrounded by barbed wire. The last phase began with the attack on Russia in 1941. At first special commando groups of the S.S., called 'Einsatzgruppen', combed the vast area from the Baltic to the Black Sea for Jews and gypsies; they killed something in the region of one million people. Then, in the autumn of 1941, the first experiments with poison gas were undertaken at Auschwitz and other concentration camps (Chelmno, Belzec, Sobibor, Treblinka, Maidanek, etc.). In Auschwitz alone, between three and four million Jews were murdered. Representatives of the various Ministries involved (including the Foreign Office) were informed of the impending 'final solution' of the 'Jewish problem' at the Berlin-Wannsee conference of 20 January 1942.

In place of emigration, a further possible solution has now begun in the shape of the evacuation of the Jews to the east, in accordance with the prior approval of the Führer.

These actions are, however, to be regarded purely as temporary expedients, although much practical experience is thereby already being gained which will prove to be most significant with regard to the coming final solution of the Jewish question. . . .

. . . In course of the final solution the Jews are to be brought to the east by suitable means in order to work. In big labour gangs, and with the sexes separated, those Jews who are capable of work will be brought to these areas and employed in road building, in which task a large part will undoubtedly fall out by natural diminution.

The remnant that is finally able to survive will, since this is unquestionably the part with the strongest capacity for resistance, have to be treated accordingly. For these people, representing a natural selection, must be seen as the germ-cell of a new Jewish reconstruction if they were allowed to go free. (See the experience of history.)

In the course of the practical execution of the final solution, Europe will be combed through from west to east.

Walther Hofer, *Der Nationalsozialismus, Dokumente 1933–1945.* Fischer Bücherei, Frankfurt, 1957, pp. 304 f.

10 The Ultimate Aim, 1941

ADOLF HITLER

In a recently discovered report of his meeting with the Japanese ambassador on 14 July 1941, Hitler revealed that when Russia had been defeated, there would be a final struggle for world domination against England and America.

The United States and England will always be our enemies. This realization must be the basis of our foreign policy. After lengthy deliberations this had become his [Hitler's] most sacred conviction, the basic principle of our future policy. America and England will always turn against whoever is in their eyes isolated. Today there were only two States whose interests could not conflict with one another, and these were Germany and Japan. America, in its new imperialist spirit, was exerting pressure alternately on the European and the Asiatic *Lebensraum*. . . . Therefore he was of the opinion that we must jointly destroy them.

Andreas Hillgruber, *Staatsmänner und Diplomaten bei Hitler*, DTV, Munich, 1969, pp. 300f.

VIII

The Aims of Hitler's German Opponents

The aristocracy was by no means the only class to oppose Hitler, but it was practically the only one which had the means to do so effectively, Most of the Weimar politicians had been either arrested or forced into exile, and what Communist or Socialist underground movements there were could proceed only by the futile and usually fatal method of seeking to win over public opinion. The dignitaries of the State – and especially those who were above suspicion because of their early support for the Third Reich – alone could organize a conspiracy, though never without the gravest personal risk. The courage of men like Stauffenberg and Oster is wholly beyond doubt. The question which must here be asked is what were the aims of the conspirators. Some German historians have represented them as 'good Europeans' and democratic idealists, but the latest research shows this to be false for most of them. Though the aims varied from group to group, there was a persistent demand for the 1914 frontier in the east (which implied the end of Poland), for Austria and the Sudetenland, for the German-speaking South Tyrol, and for colonies. If the conspirators were against Hitler in 1938 it was more because of the risky methods he was employing to achieve these aims than because of the aims themselves. In their domestic programme, most of the plotters were anything but democrats: many of the provisional constitutions they drafted gave almost absolute powers to a monarch, and relegated the representative body (in so far as allowance was made for one) to a more minor rôle than that possessed by the Imperial Reichstag. The conspirators' aims were acceptable neither to Europe nor to the German people.

1 Stauffenberg's Bomb

F. L. CARSTEN

Twenty years ago – on 20 July 1944 – officers of the High Command and the General Staff of the *Wehrmacht* which had conquered most of Europe tried to murder Hitler. But the bomb which Colonel Claus Schenck Count von Stauffenberg planted in the *Führer's* headquarters in East Prussia, while killing other participants in the staff conference held there, failed to eliminate Hitler. He was blown out of a window by the blast and escaped with slight wounds. If the conference, as was usual, had been held in an underground concrete shelter – and not in a hut above ground – not a single participant could have survived. Thus the plot failed, and the chief conspirators were executed on the same evening at army headquarters in the Bendlerstrasse in Berlin. Hundreds of others were arrested, tried, and sentenced to death by the infamous 'People's Court' or thrown into concentration camps. . . .

We know very little about Stauffenberg's political programme, for only fragments have survived his death. There is a draft of an oath which runs:

> We desire a new order that makes all Germans the bearers of the
> state and guarantees to them law and justice; but we despise the lie
> of equality and bow before the ranks created by nature. We desire
> a people that, rooted in the soil of their homeland, remains close
> to the natural forces, that finds happiness and satisfaction in working
> within its given spheres. . . . We desire leaders who, drawn from all
> ranks of the people, and linked with the divine powers, rise above
> all by their magnanimity, discipline, and sacrifice.

The sharp rebuttal of 'the lie of equality' and respect for 'the ranks created by nature' shows how far Stauffenberg's ideas were removed from those of democratic socialists. While the older generation of the conspirators aimed at a restoration of the monarchy, Stauffenberg and his friends had no real alternative to a constitutional State with its parties and trade unions. The younger officers dreamt of a society that was to be governed in a patriarchical and traditional fashion by a natural élite. In accordance with their social origin they saw this élite above all in the families of the old nobility. But would these be able to create and to guide a new state? Would the lower orders in the twentieth century be willing to accept the leadership of the nobility, especially in a country in which all ties of tradition had been destroyed by the revolution of 1918, the inflation of the early 1920s, the slump of the 1930s, and finally by Hitler's dictatorship? Apparently these questions were not discussed by the officers.

In reality the ideas of Stauffenberg and his friends – their pronounced feeling of belonging to an élite, their aristocratic attitude, their rejection of the bourgeois and the plebeian alike, their romantic and revolutionary nationalism, their emphasis on certain Prussian traditions – had, in the years before 1933, been widely discussed in the circles of 'national revolutionaries' and of the youth movement which existed outside the political parties. To anyone familiar with the atmosphere of German romantic nationalism in the 1920s, their conceptions are oddly familiar. They clearly owed much to the writings of Ernst Jünger, who at that time had been the outstanding spokesman of the 'front soldiers' of the First World War, of their longing and their mysticism, of their opposition to the new Republic and the democratic order, and of their fervent nationalism. Until 1923 Jünger was an officer of the *Reichswehr*. In his whole ideology and thought he stood very close to the younger officers, even if they were not fully conscious of this. True, Jünger later retired from all participation in political life and occupied an isolated post of observation – he knew of the conspiracy against Hitler but did not join in – yet his earlier writings continued to influence the younger generation.

This romantic and revolutionary nationalism was the spiritual background of Stauffenberg and many younger officers, a background far more familiar to them than socialism or communism, democracy or parliamentarianism. It is not surprising that their more conservative fellow-conspirators considered them revolutionaries, even revolutionaries who sympathized with the east. In reality they too stood politically on the right, but not in the camp of the traditional right-wing parties. Their ideas did not exercise any influence on the political developments in Germany after the war; but the same would have happened if the *coup d'état* which they had planned so zealously had succeeded. On their conception no new State could have been built.

'Stauffenberg's Bomb', *Encounter*, September 1964, pp. 64–7.

2 The Deportation of the Leipzig Jews

CARL GOERDELER

Goerdeler, formerly mayor of Leipzig and from 1934–5 Reich Commissar for Prices in the Hitler régime, was one of the leading figures of the German resistance to Hitler. Here he describes his horror at the deportation of the Jews.

On the 19 and 27 January [1942] Jews were again deported from Leipzig. The temperature outdoors was about minus 15 or 20 degrees centigrade. The Jews had to give up their woollen clothes and were allowed to take with them only a specified amount of luggage. They were each given a spade and then taken by open lorry – men, women and *children* – to Delitzsch, which is about 18 kilometres from Leipzig. The inhuman cruelty of this action is illustrated by the fact that the deportees included a woman of 64 whose late brother was a university professor here and who was badly wounded in the previous war, in which he received the Iron Cross First Class. From Delitzsch they were transported in cattle trucks to the east. How many of these unfortunate beings died on the way I do not know. Clearly not everyone can withstand a journey lasting several days, without heating or warm food. How many died later of tuberculosis I also do not know. But horror fills one's soul when one pictures the hearts of the fathers and mothers who watch their children dying of cold and starvation. Surely no German still capable of emotion can think that such dreadful crimes can be perpetrated without our people having to pay the penalty in the end. These crimes cannot be brought into line with the traditions of Prussian history or the history of mankind. Nothing known of man's entire past can equal such acts of deliberate and repeated cruelty. Perhaps the persecution of Christians under Diocletian was similar. People still speak of that with horror and pity, although it happened almost 2000 years ago.

But is retribution not already here, or beginning to take effect? A poor little piano teacher who had seen some of the lorries full of unhappy refugees came to see me; she was completely shattered and asked dully what retribution God had in store for the German people. Some of my friends were visited by relatives of the execution squads who said they would report sick, as they could no longer participate in such atrocities. Whoever survives this régime will learn one day what it has done to the hearts of Germans. Is it not retribution when we discover that the war in the east, which has been conducted since October according to absurd supreme orders, has already cost some 2 million men . . . ? And these are not just any members of the nation but mostly the best elements of manhood. I only know from history and from my own experience that the truth always comes out and that God always exacts just retribution.

Since this is so, we are bound by reason and honour, humanity and conscience, no longer to place German manhood at the disposal of a system which plays fast and loose with it and sacrifices it only to propel the German people in the end towards a terrible retribution and a long and harsh fate.

Vierteljahrshefte für Zeitgeschichte, Vol. 13, 1965, pp. 338–9.

3 Thoughts of a Person sentenced to Death, 1944

CARL GOERDELER

Goerdeler was no democrat. The Prussian tradition he admired most was that of Stein, Hardenberg and Bismarck. In his many draft constitutions for the new Germany he hoped to establish, he pleaded for the restoration of the monarchy, or at least for the creation of a strong presidential régime. Though he wanted a parliament with two houses, this document – drafted in September 1944 in prison, after the unsuccessful coup of July – makes it clear that this body would be dominated by 'notables', and not by men freely elected.

The district deputies elect:

(a) the district president
(b) the regional (Gau) deputies
(c) half of the 300 Reichstag deputies

The other half of the Reichstag deputies will be elected by Germans of 25 years and above in 150 election districts. The deputies must be 35 years old and have served at least five years in honorary posts in public life. For each election district, four candidates are nominated along the lines of the procedure in community elections. The candidate is chosen who receives the most votes; that means neither a proportional-representation nor a majority-vote rule. The candidates must reside in the respective election districts.

In addition to the Reichstag a Reichsständehaus will be established. To it belong:

(a) the leaders of the so-called Reichsgruppen (in the economic field)
(b) the president of the Reich Chamber of Commerce
(c) the leaders of the other national professional organizations (physicians, lawyers, officials, technicians, artists, etc.)
(d) three Protestant and three Catholic bishops
(e) the rectors of the universities
(f) a total of members of the executive boards of the German trade unions that equals the total of professional and industrial leaders envisaged (a), (b) and (c), above
(g) up to 50 respected Germans of all economic and professional sectors, who must be 50 years old and are named by the Generalstatthalter.

The government of the Reich works as a cabinet, also through resolutions under direction of the Chancellor of the Reich. Ministers who do not approve of his policy resign. The ministers are named by the Generalstatthalter. They do not require the confidence of the parliament. But he (the Generalstatthalter) must recall them if this is demanded by the Reichstag with a two-thirds majority, or by both houses with a simple majority, and provided that they name a new government at the same time.

The government can issue laws with or without agreement of the Reichstag. In the latter case it must annul the law or resign if a majority of both houses demands this, at least one of the houses by a two-thirds majority. Thus the government has a right of leadership which is not limited only to times of emergency and it has sufficient, if still controllable, possibilities of direction. It always needs the agreement of the parliament for:

(a) the budget law
(b) the tax laws
(c) treaties with foreign countries
(d) the customs laws

The two houses also can make laws by joint resolutions, but can make such laws as have financial effects not provided for in the budget only with the agreement of the government.

At the head of the State administration there will be, provisionally, a Generalstatthalter, who, after having been nominated by the government, will for the first time be elected only by the Ständehaus, as general elections are only possible after full demobilization. Term of office five years. Later election by both houses (Reichstag and Ständehaus) in common session.

It seems to me that a hereditary monarchy is the form of state for our people. Our fickle, unpolitical people needs ballast in the ship of State. The monarch shall not govern but shall watch over the constitution and represent the State. The House of Hohenzollern and the House of Wittelsbach could provide worthy monarchs, for example, Prince Friedrich, the son of the Crown Prince. If it is not possible to put a monarchy in the saddle, then things have to remain with a Generalstatthalter or a Reichspräsident who must be eligible for unlimited re-election and who after his election for the third time can also be elected for life.

Erich Zimmermann and H. A. Jacobsen, *Germans against Hitler*, published by the Press and Information Office of the Federal German Republic, Berto-Verlag, Bonn, 1960, pp. 30–1.

4 The Programme of the Kreisau Circle, 1943

The ideas of the Kreisau circle around Count Helmuth James von Moltke were less authoritarian, but they were quite unrealistic and utopian. Moltke hoped for the disappearance of the State altogether, to be replaced by 'small communities' in which the 'best' men would become the natural leaders. At the same time he assumed that there would be a profound revival of Christianity. This programme was drafted in Kreisau in August 1943.

The government of the German Reich sees in Christianity the basis for the ethical and religious revival of our people, for the conquest of hatred and lies, for the creation anew of the European community of people.

The starting-point lies in the pre-ordained contemplation by the human being of the divine order which yields to him his inner and outer existence. Only if there is success in making this order the measure of the relations between individuals and communities can the disorder of our time be overcome and a real condition of peace be achieved. The inner reorganization of the Reich is the basis for the carrying-through of a just and permanent peace.

In the collapse of a power formation which is without roots and is based exclusively on the mastery of technique, European humanity is faced with a common task. The way to its solution lies in the decisive and active implementation of the Christian substance of life. The government of the Reich is therefore determined to realize the following goals, which cannot be renounced either inwardly or outwardly, with all the means at its disposal:

1. Justice, fallen and trampled, must be restored, and must be made supreme over all orders of human life. This justice, under the protection of conscientious, independent judges who are free from fear of men, will be the basis for the future moulding of peace.
2. Freedom of faith and conscience is guaranteed. Existing laws and regulations which offend against these principles are at once abolished.
3. The casting away of the totalitarian restraints on conscience and the recognition of the inviolable dignity of the human being are foundations of the law and of the desired peaceful order of things. Everyone cooperates with full responsibility in the various social, political and international spheres of life. The right of work and property stands under public protection without regard to race, nationality or creed.
4. The basic unit of peaceful community life is the family. It stands under public protection, which shall ensure, along with education, the tangible goods of life: food, clothing, a home, a garden and health.
5. Work must be arranged in such a way that it fosters rather than stunts the enjoyment of personal responsibility. To this belongs, besides the shaping of the material conditions of work and the improvement of education in professional training, an effective co-responsibility of each person in the enterprise and beyond that in the general economic relations to which his work contributes. Thus he may co-operate in the creation of a healthy and lasting order of life, which will enable the individual, his family and the communities to

achieve their organic fulfilment within balanced spheres of economic activity. The ordering of the economy must ensure that these basic requirements are met.

6. The personal political responsibility of everyone requires his co-determining participation in the self-administration of the small and surveyable communities, which are to be revived. Rooted firmly in them, his co-determination in the State and in the community at large must be secured by self-elected representatives, and thus there must be conveyed to him a living conviction of his co-responsibility for political events in general.

7. The special responsibility and faithfulness which each individual owes to his national origin, his language, the spiritual and historical tradition of his people has to be respected and protected. However, it must not be misused for the accumulation of political power, for the degradation, persecution and suppression of foreign peoples. The free and peaceful development of national culture can no longer be made consonant with the maintenance of an individual State's absolute sovereignty. Peace means the creation of an order which encompasses the individual States. As soon as the free agreement of all peoples involved is guaranteed, the supporters of this order must also have the right to demand from each individual obedience, respect, if necessary also the risking of life and property, for the highest political authority of the community of peoples.

Erich Zimmermann and H. A. Jacobsen, *Germans against Hitler*, pp. 34–5.

5 The Foreign Aims of Hitler and his Opponents

H. R. TREVOR-ROPER

Hugh Trevor-Roper is Regius Professor of Modern History at Oxford University. In numerous publications he has argued – in sharp contrast to historians like A. J. P. Taylor – that conquest and colonization of the east was Hitler's consistent aim from the very first. In this essay, published in German translation in 1960 and printed here in the original by kind permission of the author, Professor Trevor-Roper compares Hitler's aims with those of what he calls the 'German Establishment'.

... His [Hitler's] real war was, as he so consistently stated, not a conservative war against the west but a revolutionary war against Russia.

In this matter of his real aims it was not only foreigners and historians whom Hitler deceived. He also deceived what for convenience I shall call the German Establishment. By this term I mean the German conservative civil servants and generals and politicians who, in 1933, brought him to power and who, from 1933 onwards, at least for a time, served him faithfully only to be bitterly disillusioned and sometimes, from dupes, to become martyrs: men like Neurath and Weizsäcker and Hassell and Schacht and many others. These men, I have already suggested, had war aims: or rather, political aims which might have to be realized by war, though they hoped to achieve them peacefully. They wanted, naturally, to restore German pride, shattered by defeat. They wanted to restore the army as an essential institution of State. They wanted to recover lost territory. But their territorial aims were limited: they did not want to swallow again the indigestible morsel of Alsace-Lorraine. What they wanted was land in the east only – but old lands, not new. They wanted the old imperial frontiers in Poland. If they were prepared to go a little further than the Kaiser and absorb Austria and the Sudetenland also, that was rather a necessity imposed by the Habsburg collapse than a sign of political ambitions in south-east Europe. For the demands of these men were essentially limited, essentially conservative. They might hate Russia for its Bolshevism, but they had no desire to conquer it. A war of conquest against Russia, quite apart from the cost and the risks, would entail (as Hitler himself said, it would necessitate) a German revolution. A German revolution was not wanted by the German Establishment. How then, we may ask, could the German Establishment be so mistaken as to give themselves, as indispensable agents of his policy, to a man who was not only so criminal in his methods but also so completely opposed to them in his aims?

The reasons, of course, are many. There was weakness, there was self-deception, there was subtle bribery. In many ways the German Establishment was not an establishment: it was not an aristocracy, rooted in tradition or bound together by common principles: it was a caste, an interest-group, rotted within; and Hitler exploited the rot. But also there was a hard fact of geography. One only has to look at the map of Europe to see that in order to carry out his large policy, Hitler had to begin by carrying out their small policy. Their policy was to increase German respect and self-respect by the possession of an army, in which also they were professionally interested; to knock France out of eastern Europe; and then to recover the old eastern frontiers at the expense of Poland and seal off the Habsburg gap by incorporating the Austro-Germans and the Sudeten Germans in the Reich. Then they wanted to stop. For such limited aims Hitler of course expressed nothing but contempt. He wanted to conquer Russia and occupy it permanently, up to the Urals, perhaps beyond. But how could he reach Russia except through Poland, or Poland except by detaching France? For sheer geographical reasons Hitler had to begin his revolutionary policy by carrying out the conservative policy of the establishment. This was very convenient to him. It enabled him, by playing down his ulterior aims for the time being, to buy their support. Then, when he had carried out their policy for them, he could afford to come out into the open. He was armed, victorious, unstoppable. He went on to realize his own. The full achievement of their aim was merely the essential preliminary for the achievement of his.

Thus the years 1940–1, the years of Europe's greatest crisis, were the years also of the parting of policy in Germany. It is instructive to look at the diary of Ulrich von Hassell, a perfect representative of the German Establishment, indeed its martyr. In the years before 1939 Hassell had helped to carry out Hitler's policy as ambassador in Rome, and his support of that policy, when it was revealed by the publication of the documents, shocked many westerners who, from the earlier publication of his later diaries, had come to regard him as one of themselves. But in the spring of 1940 Hassell and his friends saw all their aims realized, and they longed to make peace before the monster whose criminal genius they had used, and whom they had armed, ran amok. So they formulated their peace aims. These were 'the principle of nationality, with certain modifications resulting from history' – that is, of course, such 'modifications' as history had made in Germany's favour. In concrete terms, Hassell required 'that the union of Austria and the Sudetenland with the Reich be excluded from discussion'. 'Similarly', he added, 'the raising of the border question in the west of Germany cannot be considered, while the German – Polish border must essentially agree with the border of the German Reich of 1914'. With these 'modifications', achieved for them by Hitler, Hassell and his friends would have agreed to the 'restoration of an independent Poland and a Czech Republic'. To crown the work of conservative restoration, 'a monarchy is very desirable'.

The views of Hassell and his friends can be traced, backward and forward, in peace and war, in office and resistance, with but little variation. They are as consistent as Hitler's. They form the aspiration, the apologia, the alibi of a whole class, the burden of the documents of the *Auswärtiges Amt* in the 1930s, of the conservative resistance of the 1940s, of the self-justifying memoirs of the years after 1945. But of course they are academic, at least after 1940. Till then, these men had served Hitler; after that, they did not seriously hinder him. Power once given, once used to create its own basis, could not be taken away. And yet these men, it must be admitted, had not the excuse of foreigners. They had read, or could have read, and ought to have read *Mein Kampf*.

So Hitler set out, in 1941, to realize his permanent war-aims. Leaving the irrelevant west to its impotent, meaningless resistance, he turned east to conquer, in one brief campaign, the prize of history. After the war there were many who said that Hitler's Russian campaign was his greatest 'mistake'. If only he had kept peace with Russia, they said, he could have absorbed, organized and fortified Europe and Britain would never have been able to dislodge him. But this view, in my opinion, rests on a fallacy: it assumes that Hitler was not Hitler. To Hitler the Russian campaign was not a luxury, an extra campaign, a diversion in search of supplies or the expedient of temporary frust-ration: it was the be-all and end-all of Nazism. Not only could it not be omitted: it could not even be delayed. It was now or never that this great epochal battle must be fought, the battle which he likened to the battle of the Catalaunian Plains between Rome and the Huns. So urgent was it that Hitler could not even wait for victory in the west. That, he said, could be won afterwards: when Russia was conquered, even English obstinacy would give in: meanwhile he must strike, and strike quickly in the east.

6 Hitler's Foreign Policy

ULRICH VON HASSELL

Von Hassell was Tirpitz's son-in-law and German ambassador in Rome until 1937; shortly thereafter he became one of the leading opponents of Hitler's régime. In this passage from his diary, he discusses where his foreign aims diverged from those of Hitler.

Ebenhausen, 20 July 1943: I talked with Dieter about Hitler's foreign policy before and after the outbreak of war. I developed the following theme: the real basis of the whole catastrophic sequence is ignorance of the world, coupled with an entire lack of restraint. The political instrument was the military alliance with Italy and Japan and the consequent division of the world into two camps – moreover, in a manner which created a balance of power unfavourable to Germany.

The decisive turning-point towards war was the occupation of Prague. All preceding actions, including the *Anschluss* and the incorporation of the Sudetenland, the world had accepted. The significance of 'Munich' was that the world swallowed these events, but with a firm determination not to tolerate further German seizures without a fight.

There is absolutely no foundation for Hitler's assertion that England, after Munich, had decided to attack Germany as soon as it was strong enough. The English resolution, after they had learned their lesson and become distrustful of Hitler's assurances, was rather to improve their military position so as to be able to resist further aggressive action. It is also highly probable that had German policies been handled skilfully England would not have prevented a settlement of the Corridor question.

If it is true that Hitler later reproached Ribbentrop for having given him poor advice in proposing that he take Prague first and the Corridor later, then he was justified in the reproof. Henderson himself told me in the spring of 1939 that Prague had been the greatest disaster because it had destroyed all faith in a moderate policy and Hitler's word. If instead Hitler had taken up the question of the Corridor after a time things would probably have gone well. The seizure of Prague was all the more foolish since further developments were bound to make Czechoslovakia absolutely dependent upon Germany.

I see the errors of English policy first, in the treaties of guarantee which were bound to make Germany nervous without actually protecting the states in the east; second, that England – following a poor precedent – failed to announce with utmost earnestness at Munich that it would take military action in case the agreement was violated. All of this, of course, does not excuse Hitler's policies.

Henderson was also right when he once said that it was impossible for Hitler and Ribbentrop to maintain simultaneously two different assertions: (1) England had wanted to defeat Germany for a long time and was arming to that purpose. (2) England was decadent and weak and would not fight, therefore one could ride roughshod over England's objections. The second assertion is the one that represents Ribbentrop's actual conviction. This complete misinterpretation of the situation moved him always to fan the flames and in the decisive days of 1939 to help recklessly in bringing on the war. The historic responsibility, however, will fall on Hitler.

The Hungarian Ministers who were in Germany a short time before the outbreak of war were especially uneasy because they felt that the very cabinet officer whose special responsibility it was to weigh the facts of foreign affairs and to warn against a provocative policy worked instead most actively for a policy that inevitably led to war.

Thus these men started the war against Poland with criminal reck-lessness, risking the intervention of the western powers, completely misjudging the power relationships and, above all, without any idea at all of the significance of sea power. They thought they had created the necessary security by making a treaty with Russia, although they themselves took this step with the mental reservation which became apparent in 1941.

There is absolutely no foundation for the assertion that Russia wanted to attack, or would have attacked later. We have here the most pernicious example of the preventive war which Bismarck condemned. If Germany 'stumbled' into the two-front war in 1914, Hitler wantonly brought it on in 1941. Russia had only one feeling about an intact Germany – fear. Russia would never have attacked Germany, or at least never have attacked successfully, so long as Germany possessed an unbroken army. It suffices to imagine what would have happened if Germany, after the fall of France, had remained in possession of a fully intact, powerful instrument of war, instead of wearing it out in battle against an underestimated Russia. The fight against Russia which Hitler started was just as reckless an undertaking as the war in general. After it had started there was at least one chance – the only 'morally' good chance, from the propaganda point of view – to wage it exclu-sively against Bolshevism and to make our watchword the liberation of the Russian people, with whom Germany had no quarrel.

The opposite happened. Hitler united Russia behind Stalin against Germany. Incidentally, one might also point out the folly of aligning ourselves simultaneously against Poland as well as against Russia – a violation of the A B C of any German policy in the east.

A further ruinous decision was that of declaring war on the United States. Annoying as it was to see this power supporting the other side, it was stupid of Hitler to seize the initiative and turn the United States from a supporter of the other side into our major foe, who would use the full force of her strength against Germany. It may be that Hitler thought he owed this action to Japan. If so, it was the only instance of treaty loyalty in Hitler's career and a truly strange and disastrous one at that.

Finally there was the mistaken policy of extending the area of fighting as far as possible by the invasion of hitherto neutral territories. This procedure became the more unfortunate when the policies applied in the majority of these countries turned them into reservoirs of hatred and revenge.

In general the foreign policy of the Third Reich is characterized by a dangerous mixture of foreign and domestic considerations. The method symbolized by the names of Quisling and Mussert became especially pernicious.

The Von Hassell Diaries 1938–1944. Hamish Hamilton, London, 1948, pp. 279–81.

7 Goerdeler's Aims in 1943
CARL GOERDELER

In 1943, Germany's defeat was fast approaching, but Goerdeler – the one-time National Liberal – still believed that the Allies would accept a settlement in which all the Germans living in Europe would live in one State.

The importance of Germany's becoming sufficiently strong again follows from the necessity of securing the German Reich at least against the permanent pressure of the gigantic Russian power. This in turn involves the necessity of preserving the territorial existence of Germany that has proved reasonable and necessary through history.

Any plan to divide Germany will create repeated tensions in Germany and therefore in Europe. After all, Germany does lie in the middle of the continent. The following come into consideration as Germany's borders:

In the east: approximately the Reich borders of 1914.

In the south: the boundary recognized in the Munich conference of 1938, including Austria; moreover, South Tyrol, a purely German region, should return to Germany, up to the border of Bozen-Meran. The Italian control has only created resentment and backwardness there.

In the west: the Alsace-Lorraine question is very hard to solve. There will be no rest if Alsace-Lorraine in its old form is awarded to either Germany or France. There are two other possibilities.

(a) Alsace-Lorraine can become an autonomous country, perhaps along the lines of Switzerland.

(b) Or a neutral commission can determine the language boundary as it existed in 1918 and 1938. The French–German border could then be located between these two lines. In this second case Germany would be conceding a far-reaching self-administration to Alsace-Lorraine. . . .

In the north: the proper border with Denmark should be determined in a way similar to that followed in the west.

In any event, the internal European borders will play an ever less important part, within the European federation towards which we must strive.

This territorial continuity of the German Reich presupposes an understanding with Poland. As far as can be seen now, the continued existence of Poland depends on whether the German front in the east maintains the eastern border of Poland as of 1938. If the front collapses, Poland is lost to Russia. We understand very well the indignation and bitterness of the Polish people after all that has happened. We would feel the same. But here again a responsibility towards the future demands that such feelings be prevented from playing a prevailing rôle. They must be subordinated to orderly processes: punishment of the criminals, and restitution by cooperation. Poland can receive a substitute for West Prussia and Posnania through a federal union with Lithuania. This would benefit both peoples, and Poland would have her access to the sea. . . .

In 1918 England could accept the thoughtlessly humiliating treatment of Germany, because the might of Russia seemed to have been eliminated for a long time to come. But now Russia's recuperation cannot be doubted. Certainly Russia, too, is severely weakened by this war. But the Russian people, close to nature as they are, compensate for such losses more quickly than the more sensitive European peoples can.

At present Russia is governed by a uniformly Bolshevist system. Even the Russians cannot close their eyes to the fact that Bolshevism kills all human aspiration and endeavour. Accordingly, they have increasingly diluted Communism. But that comes only after a people under Communism has had its own bitter experience with the system. If the Russia of today gains supremacy over Europe, the central and west European peoples, weakened by war, moved by emotions, facing almost unsurmountable tasks, will fall prey to radical Bolshevism. That would be the death of European culture, and of Europe as an entity. It would also be a great danger to England. Yet Russia will be still more dangerous if she gradually finds her way back to the true laws of economics and statesmanship. For then her power will become constantly greater. Russia is the sole power on earth that can threaten the British Empire without a big fleet. It is of course England's own affair to examine this situation and then draw any conclusion that she considers to be necessary in her own interest. We can only give our opinion: that all European peoples to the west of Russia must protect themselves against Russian supremacy and hegemony.

Erich Zimmermann and H. A. Jacobsen, *Germans against Hitler*, pp. 81–2.

8 Stauffenberg's Aims, 1944

CLAUS SCHENCK VON STAUFFENBERG

After Stauffenberg's murder in July 1944, the Gestapo discovered the following memorandum on his negotiations with the British in the previous May.

1. Immediate abandonment of aerial warfare.
2. Abandonment of invasion plans.
3. Avoidance of further bloodshed.
4. Continuing function of defence strength in the east. Evacuation of all occupied regions in the north, west and south.
5. Renunciation of any occupation.
6. Free government, independent, self-chosen constitution.
7. Full cooperation in the carrying out of truce conditions and in peace preparations.
8. Reich border of 1914 in the east.
   Retention of Austria and the Sudetenland within the Reich.
   Autonomy of Alsace-Lorraine.
   Acquisition of the Tyrol as far as Bozen, Meran.

9. Vigorous reconstruction with joint efforts for European reconstruction.
10. Nations to deal with own criminals.
11. Restoration of honour, self-respect and respect for others.

Erich Zimmermann and H. A. Jacobsen, *Germans against Hitler* pp. 85–6.

9 The True Bismarck, 1944

ULRICH VON HASSELL

On a visit to the Bismarck estate of Friedrichsruh three weeks before the abortive attempt on Hitler's life, in July 1944, von Hassell took his leave of the Germany which Bismarck had created and Hitler destroyed.

I have already mentioned our visit to Friedrichsruh. On invitation of the Bismarcks we were there from Saturday evening, *1 July*, to *Monday morning, the third [1944]*. Wonderful sunny weather. It is marvellous what these two have made of Friedrichsruh – he in the park and she in the house. But everything seemed small beside the memory of the great man himself, in the house, at the crypt, in the little museum. It was almost unbearable. I was close to tears most of the time at the thought of the work destroyed.

Germany, situated in the middle of Europe, is the heart of Europe. Europe cannot live without a sound, strong heart. During recent years I have studied Bismarck, and his stature as a statesman grows constantly in my estimation. It is regrettable what a false picture of him we ourselves have given the world – that of the power-politician with cuirassier boots – in our childish joy over the fact that at last someone had made Germany a name to reckon with again. In his own way he knew how to win confidence in the world; exactly the reverse of what is done today. In truth, the highest diplomacy and great moderation were his real gifts. A picture, probably by Werner (?), portraying Bismarck as strong and forceful beside the collapsed figures of Thiers and Favre, is a good example of the foolish concept of Bismarck which we ourselves have spread abroad. This scene is quite accurately drawn, for instance the draping of Thiers' cloak. I suggested to Bismarck that the picture should be removed. Many others deserve the same fate.

The Von Hassell Diaries 1938–1944. Hamish Hamilton, 1948, pp. 316–17.

Perspectives

If one thing is clear from the foregoing selection of documents, it is that no simple definition of continuity will do justice to the complex facts of German history. Ranke's concept of continuity as 'development along a straight line', for example, is of little use even in discussing German foreign policy, where the continuity is most marked. It would perhaps be more helpful to think in terms of 'continuities' rather than 'continuity' – of a number of traditions which, like the strands of a thick rope, are intertwined but can be separated by careful analysis. There is, for instance, a striking similarity between Stresemann's demand for the restoration of the 1914 eastern frontier and the *Anschluss* of the Sudetenland, of Austria and the German parts of the South Tyrol on the one hand, and the persistent demand for the same areas by Hitler's conservative opponents after 1938. Hitler's aims were, however, far more extensive than these, and could not have been realized without general war against Russia and – for strategic reasons – the west, though not necessarily against Great Britain. Hitler's aims in turn bear a striking resemblance to the aims pursued by the Kaiser's Germany in the First World War, and particularly (as Andreas Hillgruber has emphazised) those pursued by Ludendorff in the east in 1918.[1] Here, then, are two powerful but fairly distinct traditions. How far either of them can be followed back beyond the First World War and the collapse of the Austro-Hungarian empire, is a difficult question to answer. The national liberal tradition of Stresemann and Goerdeler goes back to the *grossdeutsch* demands of the professors in the Frankfurt Assembly of 1848, and that tradition was continued (though with a different emphasis) by the Pan-Germans in the Second Reich, but at no time before the break-up of the Habsburg empire did this become official German policy. As for the Ludendorff-Hitler tradition, there were no concrete German plans for annexations in Europe before the advent of war in 1914, though it is arguable that the war aims programmes of 1914–18 were but a crystallization of the vaguer 'world

[1] See Hillgruber's brilliant essay *Kontinuität und Diskontinuität in der deutschen Aussenpolitik von Bismarck bis Hitler* (Düsseldorf, 1969).

power' dreams on the one hand and the military demand for 'security' on the other. Similarly, the task of weighing up the similarities and the differences between Germany's rôle in causing the First World War, and Hitler's part in the events leading to the Second, is a delicate and complicated one.[2]

In home affairs, the problem of continuity is more difficult still, for German history does not show that gradual evolution 'along a straight line' which is a characteristic of modern British constitutional history. It is, however, an observable fact that theories of continuity tend to arise not in connection with countries where historical continuity is self-evident, but rather where, as in the case of France, Russia and Germany, there has been rapid and revolutionary change. Adherents of the continuity view then claim that *despite* the upheaval, certain features remained constant, or changed less rapidly than others. A classic example is Alexis de Tocqueville's argument that the Jacobin régime and the Napoleonic dictatorship merely continued the work of centralizing and modernizing France begun by the *ancien régime*. Adolf Hitler himself gave expression to a view very commonly held in the west, when he said: 'Stalin pretends to have been the herald of the Bolshevik revolution. In actual fact, he identifies himself with the Russia of the Tsars, and he has merely resurrected the tradition of Pan-Slavism'. It is because of this paradoxical nature of the idea of continuity in such cases that the German historian, Gustav Adolf Rein, has suggested that the Hegelian concept of the dialectic might serve as a more useful model than the Rankean idea of the straight line.[3] In this view, Napoleon would be the 'synthesis' of the autocracy of the *ancien régime* and the democracy of the Revolution, and Stalin the 'synthesis' of Tsarism and the Russian Revolution. Applied to German history between 1871 and 1945, this would mean seeing the Bismarckian Reich as the 'thesis' (though itself a 'synthesis' of earlier contradictory forces), the Weimar Republic as the 'antithesis' which had been growing beneath the surface of the Empire to burst through in the revolution of 1918, and Hitler's Third Reich as the 'synthesis' between the old authoritarianism and the new forces of popular nationalism. Continuity would be provided by the fact that each stage is the 'logical' and 'necessary' product of its predecessor.

[2] A. Hillgruber, *Deutschlands Rolle in der Vorgeschichte der beiden Weltkriege* (Göttingen, 1967).

[3] G. Adolf Rein, 'Zum Problem der historischen Kontinuität', in *Jahrbuch der Ranke-Gesellschaft*, 1955, pp. 14f.

In the realm of ideas, Rein advances the concept of 'underground continuity', but this too raises problems. In particular, this concept conflicts with that of 'surface continuity' – between the aims pursued by the men actually in power – which we have been studying in this book. Friedrich Ebert's metaphor of 1919, that the spirit of Goethe and Schiller, Lassalle and Marx, Fichte and the men of 1848, had passed over the Second Reich 'in crane-like flight', is a good illustration of this conflict. So, too, is the attempt of modern historians to trace Nazi ideology back into the past. Paul de Lagarde, it is widely agreed, expressed ideas in the mid-nineteenth century which had much in common with later Nazism; but he expressed those ideas in direct and conscious opposition to the limited and comparatively liberal Bismarckian Reich, and Bismarck abhorred such sentiments. Thus, by tracing a line from Lagarde to Hitler we would, in a sense, be denying the existence of a similar link between Bismarck and Hitler.

In the last analysis, seeing continuity in history means seeing things from a certain distance. To most Germans living through the upheavals of 1918, it seemed as if a world was coming to an end. Only with the wisdom of hindsight can the historian discern that the change was less fundamental than contemporaries supposed, that the thrones fell but the old army, the old bureaucracy, the old university professors, the old party leaders, the old internal boundaries, remained. Only with the wisdom of hindsight can we say, as James Joll does, that Rathenau's beliefs were similar to those held by his assassins, or, as Hans Mommsen does, that Hitler and the men who tried to kill him in July 1944 had common spiritual roots in the youth movement, the years in the trenches, in Nietzsche's philosophy and neo-Kantianism. Only from the perspective of the distant observer do Bethmann Hollweg's aims in the First World War seem to coincide largely with those of Ludendorff, who overthrew him, or Stresemann's with those of Seeckt, who came close to so doing. That there is a certain arbitrariness in thus stressing the similarities and discounting the differences, cannot be denied, nor that that arbitrariness might be accentuated by the method, used here, of illustrating the controversy by means of selected documents. One can only hope to persuade the reader that this is, in Alexander Gerschenkron's words, 'the arbitrariness of the process of cognition' which has 'nothing to do with the arbitrariness of a meaningless political slogan'.[4]

[4] A. Gerschenkron, 'On the Concept of Continuity in History', in *Continuity in History and other Essays* (Cambridge, Mass., 1968) p. 38.

Index